The Confederacy's Secret Weapon

The Confederacy's Secret Weapon

The Civil War Illustrations of Frank Vizetelly

Douglas W. Bostick

The History Press

Published by The History Press
Charleston, SC 29403
www.historypress.net

First published 2009

Manufactured in the United States

ISBN 978.1.59629.592.6

Library of Congress Cataloging-in-Publication Data

Bostick, Douglas W.
The Confederacy's secret weapon : the Civil War illustrations of Frank Vizetelly / Doug Bostick.
p. cm.
Includes bibliographical references and index.
ISBN 978-1-59629-592-6 (alk. paper)
1. Vizetelly, Frank, 1830-1883. 2. United States--History--Civil War, 1861-1865--Journalists. 3. United States--History--Civil War, 1861-1865--Press coverage. 4. United States--History--Civil War, 1861-1865--Art and the war. 5. Confederate States of America--Press coverage. 6. War correspondents--United States--History--19th century. 7. War correspondents--Great Britain--History--19th century. 8. Engraving, British--19th century. 9. Illustrated London news I. Title.
E609.B676 2009
973.7'84--dc22
2009026256

This book is dedicated to my son, Brooks Bostick, who shares many of the qualities and attributes of Frank Vizetelly. In addition to their artistic interests, they share inquisitiveness and a sense of fascination with the challenges before them. Like Vizetelly was, Brooks is an affable person who lights up any room he enters. Some suggest that a person's greatest legacy is the children one brings into this world. If that is true, my life has been a great success!

Contents

Acknowledgements

Raised in Charleston, I was taught the importance of history residing in a city steeped in centuries of fascinating stories. As a teenager, I became aware of woodcut engraving and the illustrated newspapers published during the Civil War. Schindler's Antique Shop on King Street in Charleston was the first business that appreciated the public's interest in the fascinating engravings found in the pages of *Harper's Weekly*, *Frank Leslie's Illustrated News* and the *Illustrated London News*.

The artists that sketched for these important newspapers allowed nineteenth-century readers to *see* the news of the day. These illustrated newspapers were the CNN of their time. During the Civil War, photography was available only to the elite who could pay to visit the expensive New York photographic parlors. War correspondents like Frank Vizetelly, William Waud, James Taylor and Thomas Nast made the images of the war accessible to the public. They influenced both the way in which the public understood the war and many of the social and cultural icons of the day. Nast's images of Santa Claus became the jolly elf image that has been perpetuated through to the twenty-first century.

I am indebted to bookstores and antique shops from Washington, D.C., to San Diego that have allowed me to rummage through their old collections of engravings for purchase. Many thanks to Timothy Hughes Rare & Early Newspapers for its resources, educational offerings and vast collection of collectable newspapers for sale.

Special thanks to the Lewis H. Beck Center of the Emory University Library. In 1988, work began on a project (completed in 2000) to scan and preserve the complete text and image collection of the *Illustrated London News* as it pertained to the American Civil War. Its work was invaluable in making this story accessible.

Acknowledgements

Thank you to The History Press for its understanding of this subject and supporting the proposal to bring this lost story to print.

Thank you to my family for their understanding and support. I owe a special thanks to my son Brooks who spent many hours assisting me in organizing and scanning my collection of old and historic newspapers.

It is my hope that Frank Vizetelly, a gregarious and talented Englishman, finds his deserved place in our history. He, after all, spent a career trying to present and preserve it for us.

Introduction

By 1860 in America, news traveled faster than at any other time in history thanks to fifty thousand miles of telegraph wire that crossed the nation and the proliferation of newspapers. By the time of the firing on Fort Sumter in April 1861, there were four newspapers in the world that featured woodcut engravings and could produce them quickly while the news was still topical: the *Illustrated London News* in England and *Harper's Weekly*, *Frank Leslie's Illustrated Newspaper* and the *New York Illustrated News*, all published in New York.

The *Illustrated London News,* the first and oldest of the illustrated newspapers, was founded in 1842 by Herbert Ingham and Henry Vizetelly. Vizetelly noticed a strong following for cheap London papers like the *Observer* and the *Weekly Chronicle*, which featured several small woodcut engravings. Additionally, whenever these engravings appeared on the front page, sales increased.

Ingham and Vizetelly conceived of a newspaper that would be sixteen pages in length and feature thirty-two engravings per issue. The first issue on May 14, 1842, sold 26,000 copies. Their illustrated newspaper was sought the world over by readers wanting to see the images of the biggest news stories of the time. The popularity soared as the newspaper reached out to cover news across the world. By 1863, the circulation for the *Illustrated London News* reached 300,000, compared to only 70,000 for England's foremost daily newspaper, the *London News*.

The illustrated newspapers employed their own artists and correspondents but also bought sketches of topical news from many other artists, writers, engineers and military men from around the world. However, the drawing or sketch itself was only the first step in getting an image to the street in the newspaper.

After the sketch arrived at the newspaper office, it was redrawn, if needed, to provide greater detail. The detailed drawing was then rubbed in reverse on a block of Turkish boxwood. The wood of the Turkish boxwood tree was favored because it would not splinter and could hold fine lines in the carving.

The next step was to enhance the image with India ink and pencil to provide the final image for carving. A beeswax mold of the carving was made and then immersed in an electro-charged bath to cause a copper coating to adhere to the mold. The thin copperplate was used to print the newspapers.

Frank Vizetelly, Henry's younger brother, was one of the world's first war correspondents. He loved the action and drama of war, knowing that it made for great news and great illustrations. By 1860, Vizetelly was already a seasoned war correspondent, covering engagements in France, Austria, Italy and the Mediterranean Islands. As America moved headlong into war, Vizetelly was covering Giuseppe Garibaldi and the Second Italian War of Independence.

Vizetelly was raised in a literary family. His father managed Vizetelly, Branston & Company, a London publishing house. His brothers Henry and James were journalists. Vizetelly was raised with the intelligentsia of England and France. He counted Gustave Dore, the renowned French artist, and William Blanchard Jerrold, the famed British playwright, among his closest friends.

Chapter 1

The Bon Vivant Arrives

Europe followed the growing tensions in the United States as the North and the South raced toward an armed conflict over the right to secede. While everyone in Europe had an opinion over the schism between the slaveholding states in the South and the Northern states, the primary concern in Europe was over access to the raw products produced in the South—principally cotton.

While Frank Vizetelly was still in Italy, Sir William Howard Russell of the London *Times*, Francis C. Lawley of the London *Telegraph* and Percy Greg of the London *Standard* were already in America writing about the War of the Rebellion. In the spring of 1861, Henry Vizetelly hired his brother Frank to cover the American Civil War for the *Illustrated London News*.

After the firing on Fort Sumter, the *Illustrated London News* featured a weekly column entitled "The Civil War in America." In the first few months of the war, the newspaper bought illustrations from several correspondents in America before deciding to send their own reporter. Interestingly, the newspaper first referred to the conflict as the "American Revolution of 1861."

Vizetelly was anxious to get to America, fearing that the war could end quickly. The *Illustrated London News* published an interview with Cassius Clay, United States minister to St. Petersburg, in which he asserted, "The whole seven revolted states have not as much white population as the single state of New York. We can blockade them by sea, and invade them by land, and close up the rebellion in a single year if we are let alone."

Vizetelly booked passage in Liverpool for the twelve-day trip bound for Boston. While aboard his ship the *Europa*, he was busy musing about the war and his role in covering it. With several wars under his belt, Vizetelly referred to himself as an "old traveler…used to knocking about the world." He had a reputation for becoming part of the stories he covered. Many

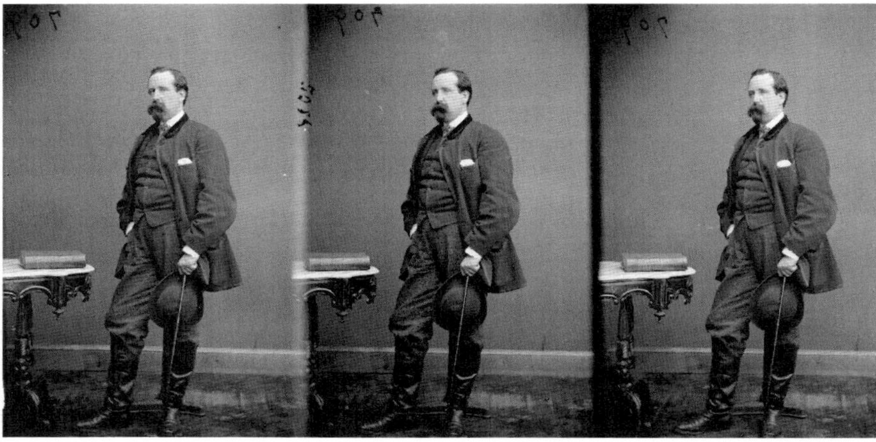

Frank Vizetelly, war correspondent for the *Illustrated London News*. *Courtesy of the Library of Congress.*

traveling correspondents preferred to cover armed conflicts from the sidelines. Vizetelly, however, always chose to be in the middle of the action, on the field of battle and riding with the troops.

Despite the need to "rough it" while encamped with Garibaldi's army, Vizetelly loved the comforts and finer things of life. One writer referred to Vizetelly as "irrepressible, a sprawling, gregarious bon vivant."

Once he arrived in Boston, Vizetelly quickly updated himself on the latest news across the country as he measured where he should insert himself to effectively cover the war. In his first report filed with London, he noted, "The latest news for the States is of very warlike character…The forward movement of national troops on Baltimore has commenced. Large bodies of troops from the South are also advancing into Virginia. Senator Wigfall has announced that 100,000 Southerners are on their way to Washington."

Vizetelly's reports read like his own journal, recording not only the news as he found it but also his impressions and opinions. He wrote:

> *On landing at Boston, I was surprised at the enthusiasm displayed by the people of the North after what I heard in England of their apathy. Everywhere the Stars and Stripes of the Union floated in the breeze, while every man wore a patriotic badge in his buttonhole…*
>
> *Nor is it surprising that a population whose forefathers were the first to assert their independence should rise en masse to preserve the integrity of the Constitution of which their ancestors laid the foundation…*

Boston was the first to unfurl the national flag, and Boston should be the last to see it hauled down.

Vizetelly quickly made his way by train to New York and, again, was surprised in his observations. From New York, he filed his second report and the first of his illustrations:

I could easily believe myself to be in Paris or some other city devoted to military display, instead of New York, the commercial emporium of the North. From morning to night nothing is heard but the sound of drum or the martial strains from trumpet and bugle, as regiment after regiment passes on its way to the seat of war through streets crowded with a maddened population. All trade is at a standstill. Store after store down Broadway has been turned into the head-quarters of Anderson's Zouaves, Wilson's Boys, the Empire City Guard, and hosts of corps too numerous or too eccentric in their names for me to recollect. Verily, a cosmopolitan army is assembled here. As one walks he is jostled by soldiers dressed in the uniforms of the Zouaves de la Garde, the Chasseurs a' Pied, Infanterie de la Ligne, and other French regiments—so great, apparently, is the admiration of our cousins for everything Gallic. I must confess I should prefer to see more nationally. Injustice, however, to the men, I cannot do otherwise than express my unqualified approval of the material out of which the North is to make her patriotic army. Many of those I have seen marching through the streets appear already to have served in the field, so admirably do they bear themselves in their new roles. The very children have become tainted with the military epidemic, and little toddling Zouaves, three and four years old, strut, armed to the teeth, at their nurses' apronstrings. As I write I have a corps of chasseurs composed of all the small boys in the hotel exercising and skirmishing in the corridor outside my room; the shrill words of command from the juvenile Colonel pierce through and through my ears, and distract my attention terribly.

There is not a house that does not display Union colours of some kind; there is not a steeple ever so lofty that it is not surmounted by a star-spangled banner; there is not a man or woman in the city that does not wear a patriotic badge of some kind. It is a mighty uprising of a united people determined to protect their flag to the last. In a future letter I shall enter into the merits of this quarrel, as I may be able to ascertain them, which now divides two branches of the same family.

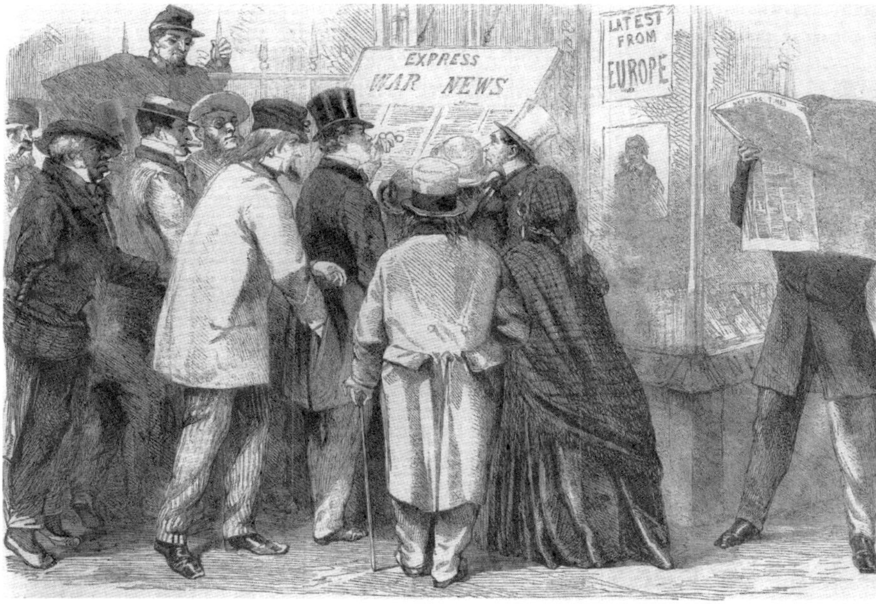

War news in New York.

News of the war was posted daily for New Yorkers to ponder. Many of the city's volunteer fire companies reformed their units into regiments that offered their services for the war. Vizetelly noted, "The fire-brigades, composed of picked men of the city, are, in fact, well-organized clubs, and their stations are fitted up with reference to the tastes and habits of such associations…its immediate attention is the numerous placards which have reference to the civil war now unhappily impending."

Vizetelly spent considerable time visiting with the many regiments forming in New York and making ready to embark down south. Many of these regiments made temporary quarters in makeshift shanty towns until they received their orders. In sketching "Wilson's Boys" in camp, Vizetelly remarked, "This corps might properly be styled the 'Chevalier Guard,' being composed of the chevaliers d'industrie of New York; They have no regular uniforms yet, though I do not know but what their present costume is the most picturesque."

The scene repeated itself day after day in New York as troops marched through Broadway to city hall, where they were reviewed before making their way through White and North Moore Streets to the piers to board a waiting ship for transport. Vizetelly recorded, "The march through Broadway was an ovation, the splendid appearance of the men eliciting the most enthusiastic cheers and demonstrations of satisfaction from the multitude that lined the sidewalks and filled the windows along the route."

Vizetelly traveled farther south to Washington with a regiment of the New York Firemen Zouaves, commanded by Colonel Ellsworth. In Washington, he first visited the British embassy, where he met with Lord Edmund Lyons, the British ambassador to the United States, and Russell, the correspondent with the *Times.*

While Vizetelly was waiting for official clearance as a foreign observer, he often attended "private theatricals" at the embassy in the company of Lord Lyons and, on occasion, President Lincoln.

By May 31, Vizetelly was in Northern Virginia covering the movements and preparations of the Union army. He was with the New York Firemen Zouaves as they crossed the Potomac River to Alexandria. On reaching the Virginia city, he witnessed the first in a long line of tragic loss of life:

> [The night] *was marked by a sad event—the assassination of a young man of great promise, who had already achieved fame—Colonel Ellsworth. He was shot by the proprietor of a hotel as he was carrying downstairs a*

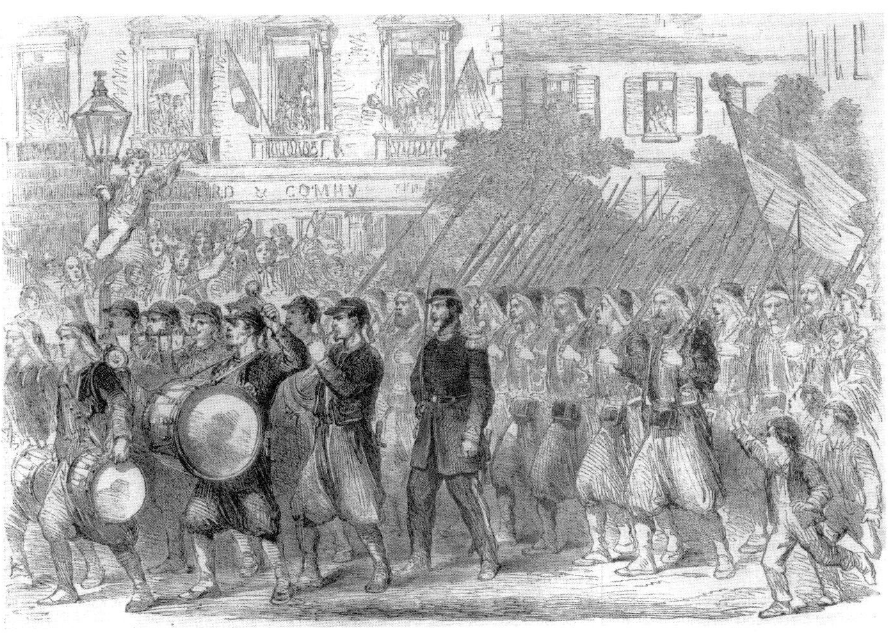

The Fifth Regiment of the New York Zouaves.

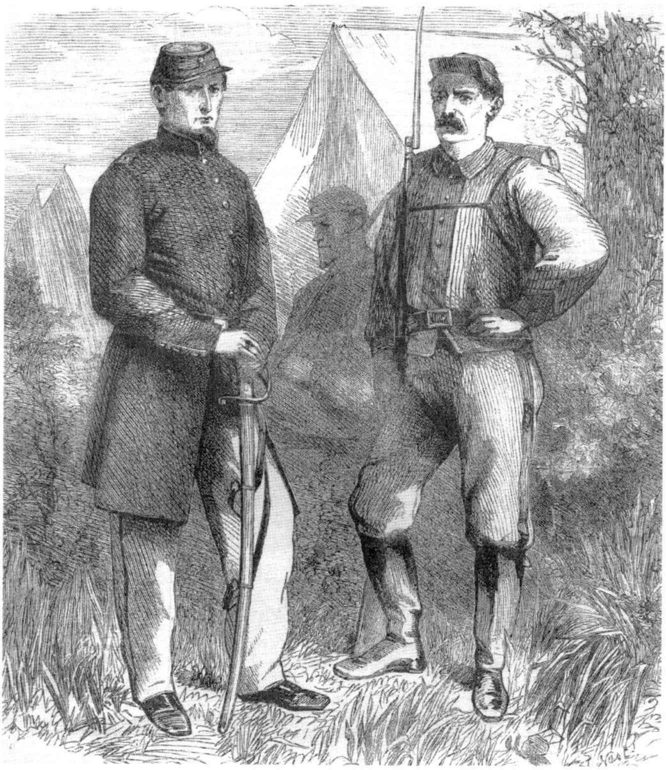

New York Firemen Zouaves, with Colonel Ellsworth (left).

Secession flag. His regiment was at once wild with rage, and it was with difficulty it was prevented from burning the town. The assassin was killed on the spot. Colonel Ellsworth was a man of much force of character, and of especial genius for organization and military drill; he was, in fact, the originator of the Zouave drill in the United States. When the war began it occurred to him that the firemen of New York would furnish excellent material for a military corps of this description; he at once proposed the matter, and, the consent of the authorities being given, a regiment was immediately formed and conveyed to Washington. In a sort of reckless courage this class of men have hardly their equals anywhere. The skill of Colonel Ellsworth soon added the advantages of skill and discipline, and the force had already become as formidable a one as any in the field. He was greatly loved by his men, and seems to have been a man of exemplary life.

Chapter 2

PROBING THE ENEMY

By early June, Vizetelly chose to camp with the Second New York Regiment just outside of Washington. From this base of operations, he was able to observe the buildup and organization of the Federal army at the nation's capital. By June 1861, Union forces in Washington totaled more than sixty thousand troops. General Scott had an additional fifteen to twenty thousand troops across the Potomac River in Virginia between Alexandria and Arlington Heights.

While encamped with the Second New York, Vizetelly sketched the two principal bridges connecting Washington to Virginia: the Long Bridge and the Chain Bridge at Georgetown. The Long Bridge, a drawbridge, was guarded by several units of Federal artillery. At night, the bridge was raised to provide for better security.

Aware that Federal troops were organizing at Washington, slaves from Virginia plantations frequently escaped their masters to seek protection at the Union camps. Once the authorities could establish that their masters were secessionists, the slaves were treated as contraband of war.

The growing Union army in Washington prepared for a grand celebration on Independence Day 1861, with a large parade planned. More than twenty thousand troops participated. President Lincoln, General Winfield Scott and other dignitaries gathered in the official review stand. Vizetelly sketched the Garibaldi Guard as they passed President Lincoln in review. The guard was made up of Hungarians, Germans, Swiss, Italians and French in uniforms styled after the Sardinian Bersaglieri in Europe. Each man was adorned with fresh green sprigs, which they tossed toward General Scott in respect as they passed.

The early summer of 1861 was marked by both armies, only miles apart, probing each other to determine strength, position and response tendencies.

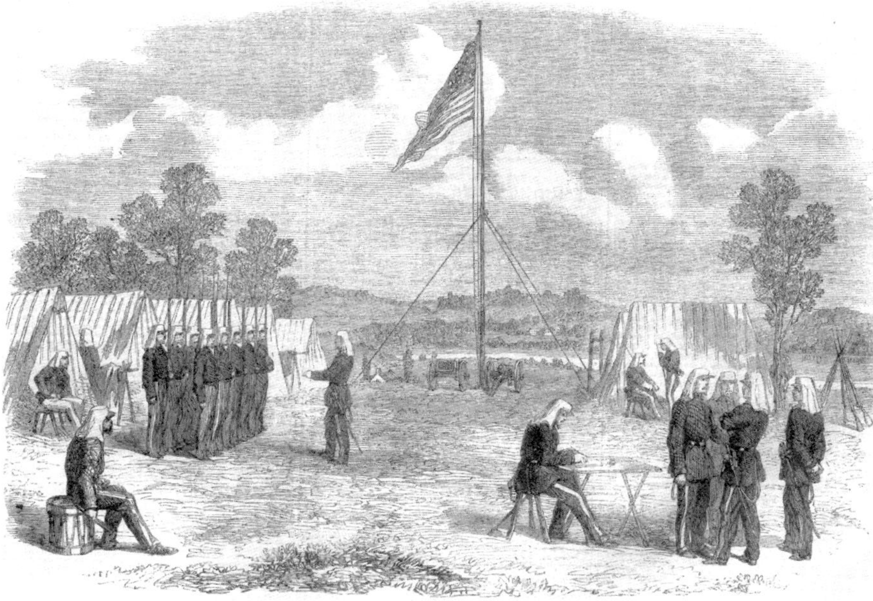

Vizetelly's campsite near Washington.

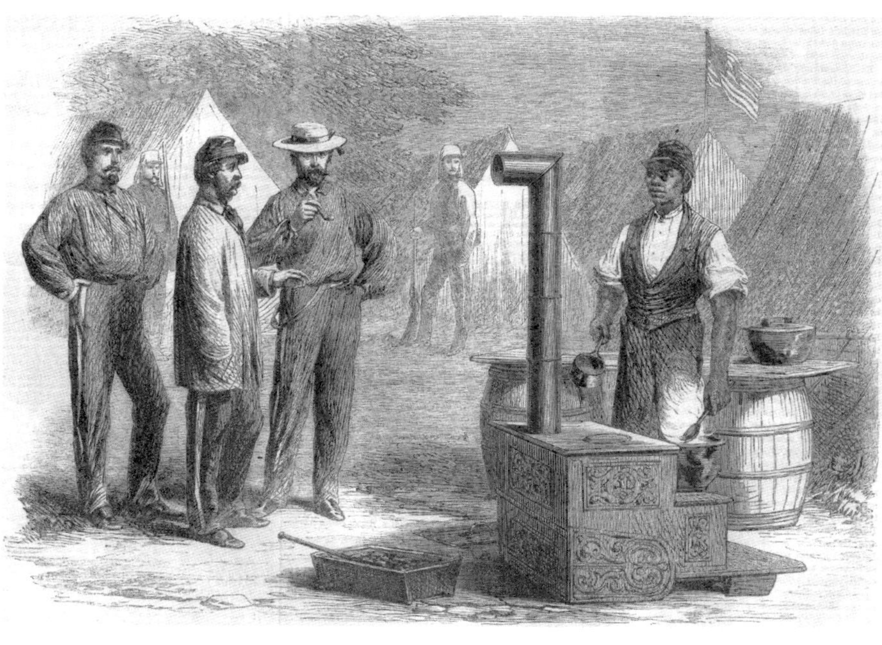

The kitchen operation for the Second New York Regiment.

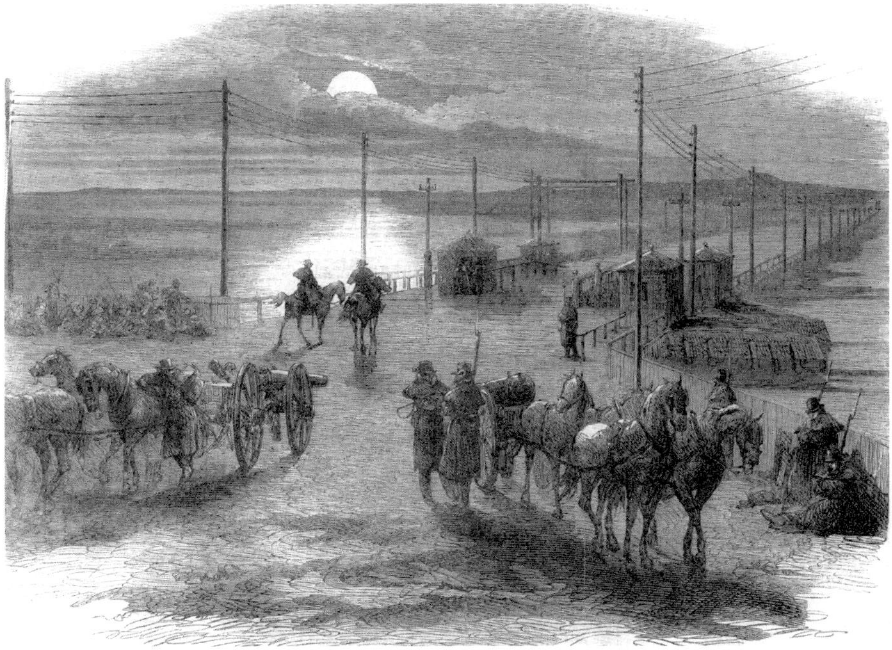

The Long Bridge over the Potomac at Washington.

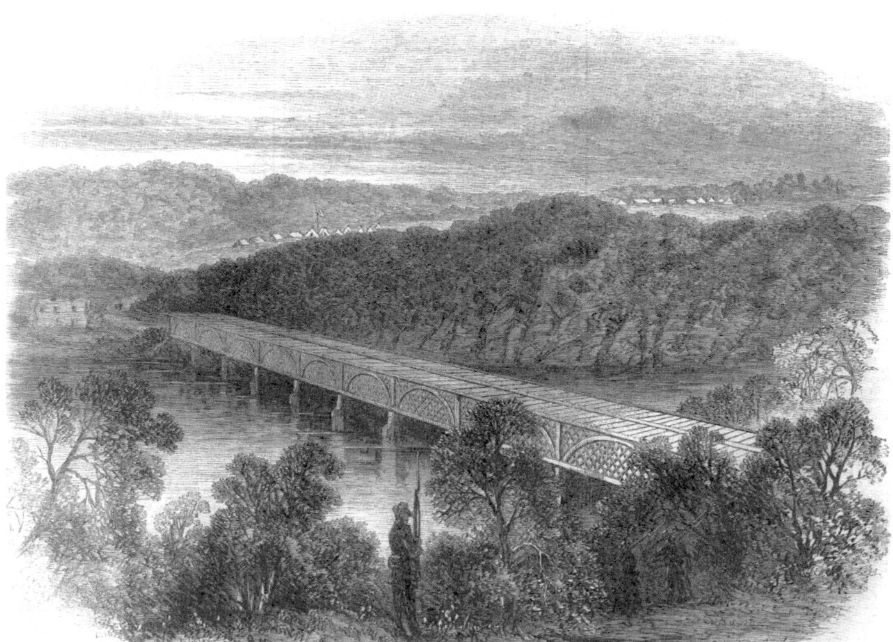

The Chain Bridge at Georgetown.

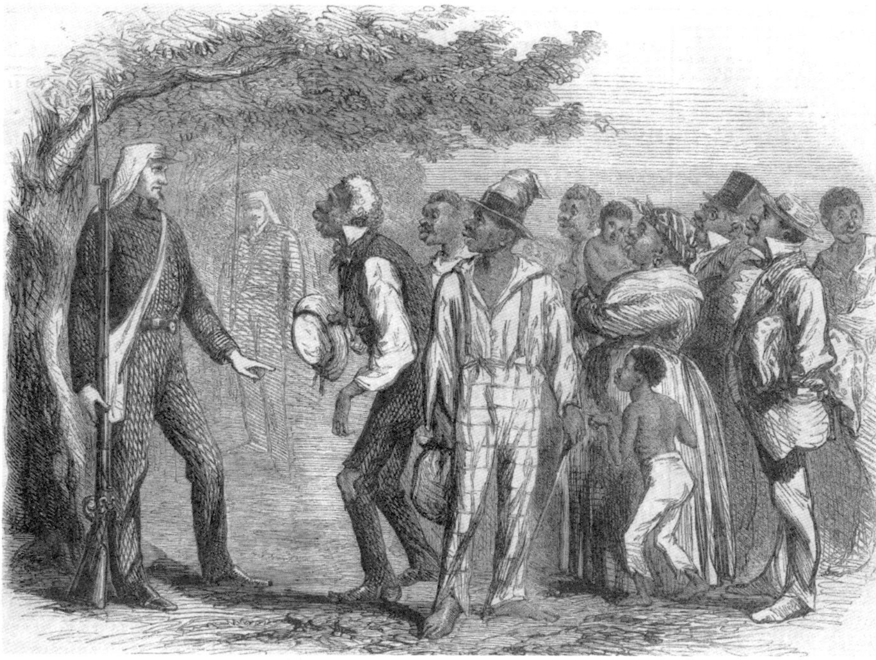

Contraband of war.

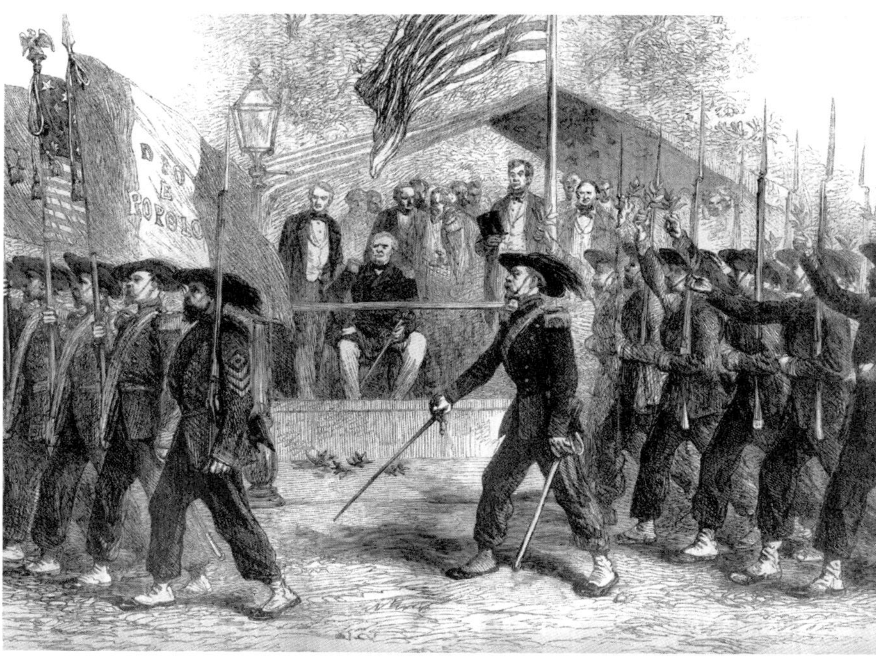

Review of the troops by President Lincoln and General Scott on Independence Day 1861.

In Northern Virginia, the Federal army was centered at Alexandria. The Confederate stronghold was located seventeen miles to the west in Fairfax. Both armies routinely sent patrols and reconnaissance parties to the countryside between the two towns.

Picket duty overnight was particularly hazardous, as it was common to find yourself facing a scouting party from the opposing army. Vizetelly noted in one report, "The sentry duty at the front of the Unionist camp is, we are told, exceedingly hazardous and very few of those who are posted at night expect to see another day dawn."

Vizetelly reported further:

> *Charges of brutality, and even assassination, are rife in the Unionist camp against the Secessionists, who, doubtless, have countercharges with which they also could horrify us, had they, like their rivals, the ears of Europe; for all the camps are sure to be infested with desperadoes who, under the garb of Patriotism, prowl about to gratify their own evil purposes…The country all round is thickly covered with wood, and in the darkness the Secessionists, acquainted with every cowpath, creep softly towards the poor fellow pacing to and fro on the road, taking advantage of every shadow, and profiting by*

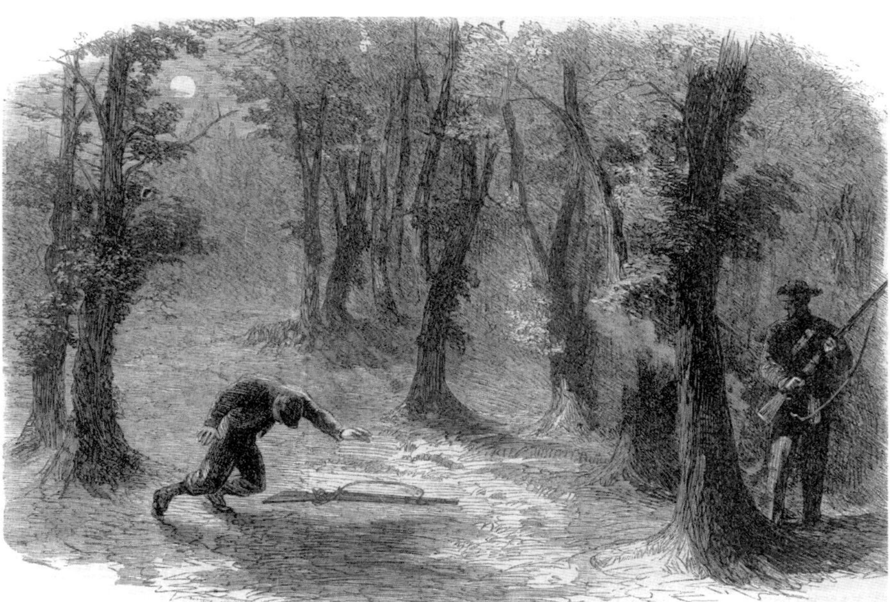

Federal sentry killed by Confederates.

the rustle of every falling leaf, until close upon him, where either the bowie-knife or a rifle-shot does the rest.

These scouting parties accounted for most of the action in the early summer. Always anxious to be at the epicenter of any action, Vizetelly frequently accompanied the Union patrols. On one such occasion, he sketched himself in the center of an illustration of a night scouting party that ventured out twelve miles through the country but did not encounter the enemy. He reported, "The men were dressed in round slouched hats, rough flannel blouses, and carried revolvers and bowie-knives in their belts."

Over the next month, Vizetelly traveled with many of the patrols between Alexandria and Fairfax. He accompanied a cavalry patrol that did attack a force of Confederates at Fairfax Court House. He reported that the secessionists had casualties of twenty-seven compared to only six for the Union cavalry.

Cloud's Mill was a gristmill near Alexandria where Union troops gathered for their provisions. While visiting the mill in late June, Vizetelly and the Union troops were surprised by a group of "Confederate Guerilla horsemen." They rode into the troops, surrounded a Union officer and carried him off, presumably to gather intelligence.

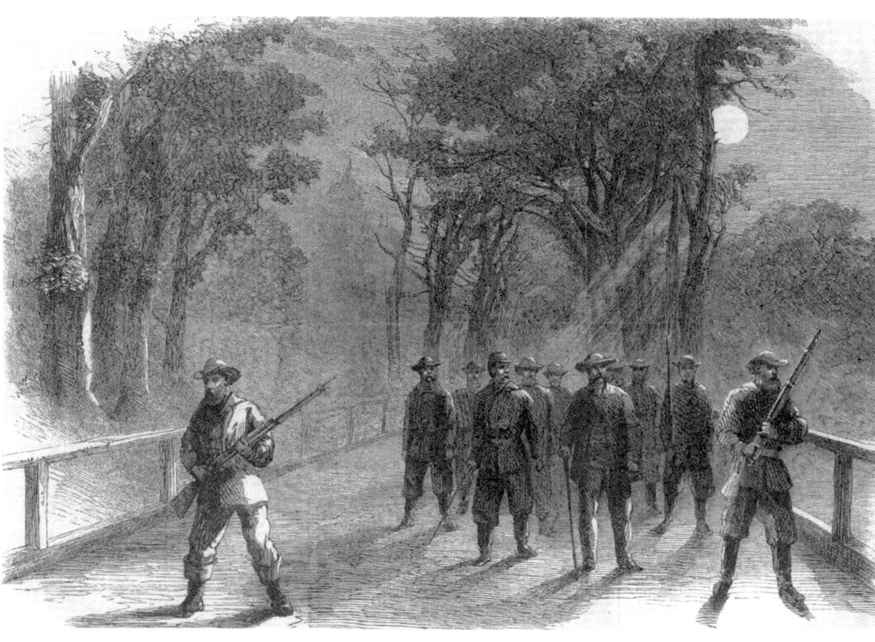

Federal scouting party patrolling at night near Alexandria.

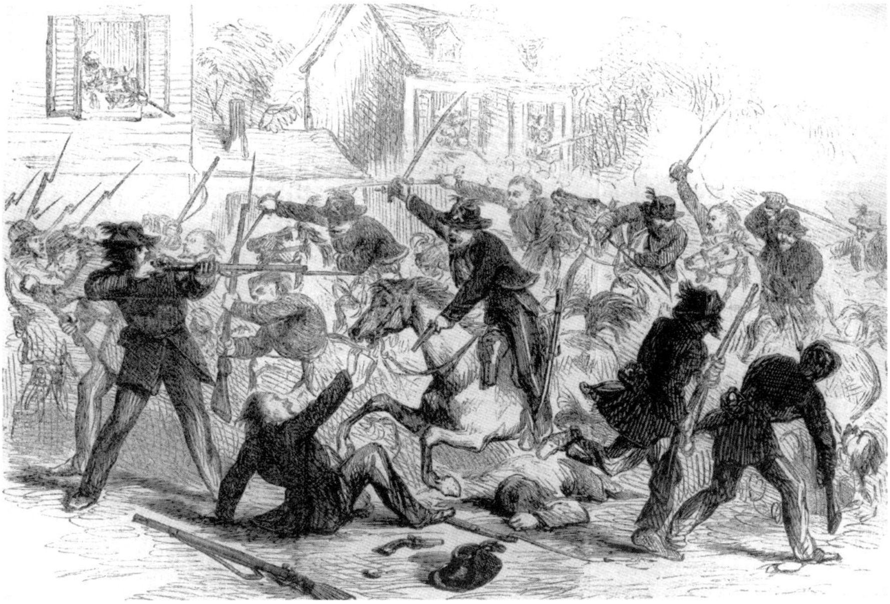

Charge of the Federal cavalry at Fairfax Courthouse.

Vizetelly continued to spend his time with several of the New York regiments encamped around Washington and Virginia. He often encamped with the Garibaldi Guard. He was a welcomed visitor, as he enthralled them with his stories of covering the Garibaldi campaign in Italy and Sicily for the newspaper. On one occasion, a Confederate scouting party crossed the river under darkness and fired upon the Garibaldi pickets.

In midsummer, Vizetelly accepted an invitation to ride on the *Resolute*, a picket boat that patrolled the Potomac River. On one patrol, the lookouts spotted a scow loaded with barrels on the Virginia shore of the river yet there were no people at the scene and no activity of any kind. Thinking that the barrels were likely filled with gunpowder smuggled by Confederates, the captain launched a small boat and crew to recover the contents of the scow.

They did not appreciate that this could have been a Confederate trap. As the small boat neared the shoreline "a murderous fire was opened from behind the bushes on the bank." All but one of the crew were either killed or wounded before the *Resolute* could open fire and withdraw.

Keeping such large numbers of troops in provisions was no small task. In one of his reports, Vizetelly described the process of killing bullocks (young bulls) in camp:

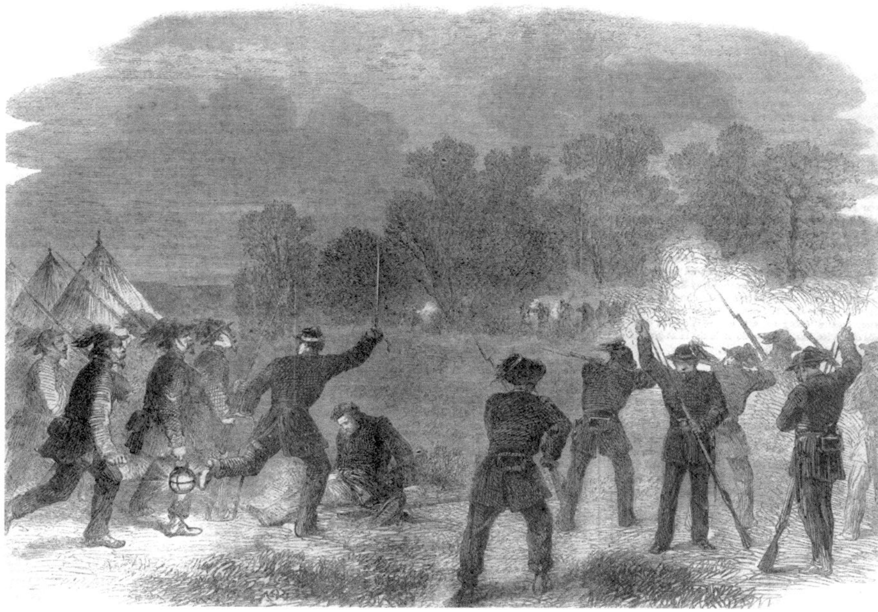

Attack on the pickets of the Garibaldi Guard on the east branch of the Potomac River.

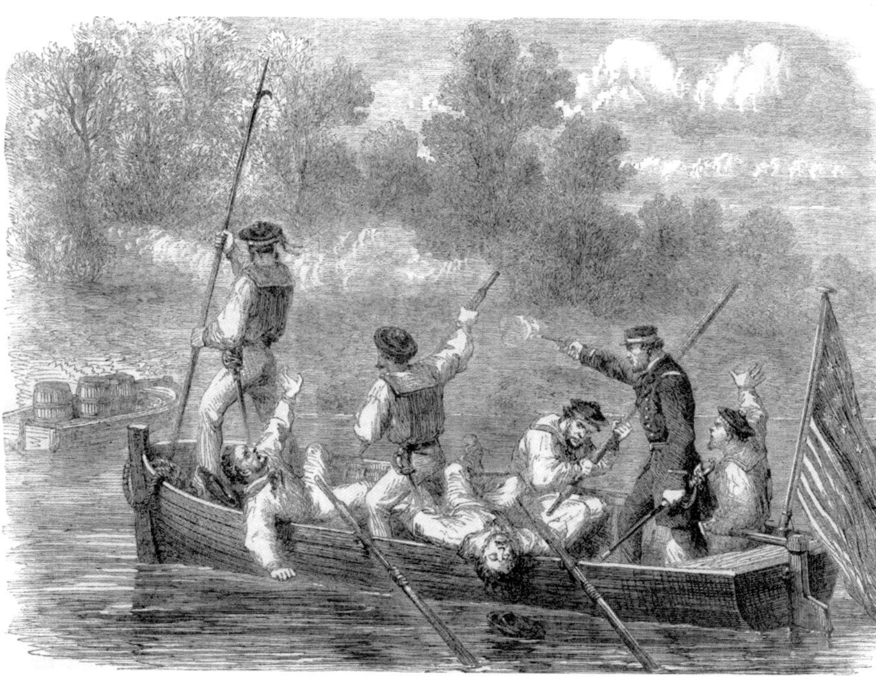

A trap set by the Confederates.

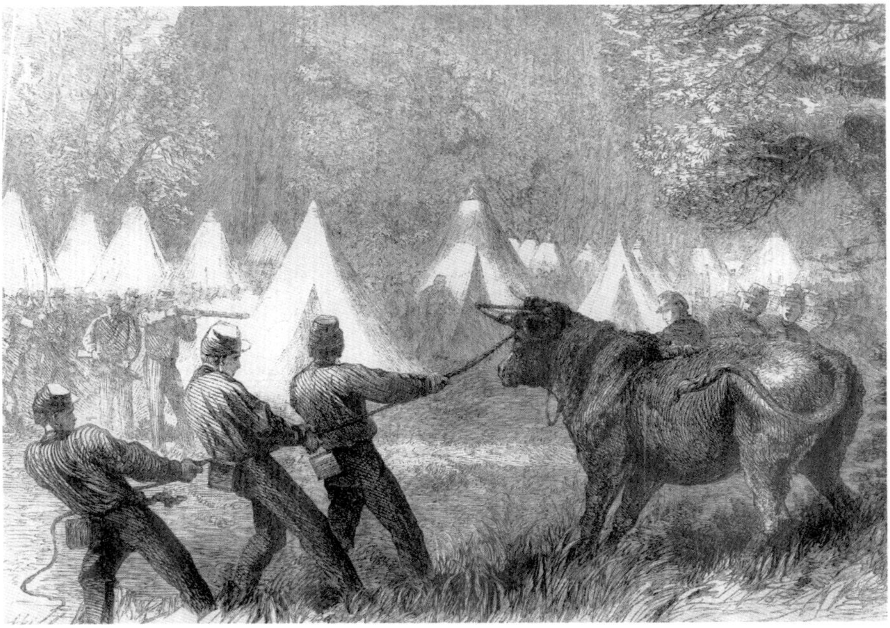

The quartermaster's department killing a bullock in the Federal camp.

The regiments encamped at a distance from the Commissariat Storehouse in the Federal camp get their fresh meat delivered to them alive, a bullock being unceremoniously turned into the canvas streets for them to slaughter, cut up, and prepare as they may think fit. The fashion of dispatching the beast is usually as follows: Lassos are thrown over its horns and made fast, when three or four men on each side hang on with all their strength and steady the animal's head. Some of the best shots in the regiment are then chosen, and one advances, takes deliberate aim at the forehead, and, if successful, the poor brute rolls over dead. Should he, however, simply wound it, those who have hold of the ropes have a rough time of it, being dragged about the field until the animal is again secured, when another marksman steps forward, and generally finishes the work.

Chapter 3

Trouble at Manassas Junction

General Irvin McDowell was named by President Lincoln as commander of the Army of Northeastern Virginia, though he had never commanded troops in combat. Immediately, he received pressure from Lincoln and Washington politicians to march on the newly established Confederate capital at Richmond, Virginia.

There were three Confederate armies in Virginia by early July 1861. General P.G.T. Beauregard, a classmate of McDowell's at West Point, was encamped at Manassas Junction with approximately twenty thousand troops. General Joseph Johnston was in the Shenandoah Valley with twelve thousand troops, and General Holmes was on the lower Potomac River with three thousand troops.

McDowell dispatched Union general Robert Patterson with 3,500 men to attack the division under Johnston to keep them from reinforcing Beauregard. McDowell then planned to advance on Beauregard at Manassas.

Colonel Thomas Jackson, commanding a brigade under Johnston, was north of Martinsburg. On July 2, Jackson learned that Patterson's men had crossed the Potomac heading south and ordered the Fifth Virginia Regiment with only 380 men and one cannon to confront the advancing Union troops at the Porterfield Farm at Hainsville.

Utilizing the heavily wooded area to disguise its real strength, the Fifth Virginia engaged the Union force for forty-five minutes before retreating to avoid being surrounded. Lieutenant Colonel J.E.B. Stuart's cavalry surprised and captured forty-nine Union soldiers during the fight.

Despite the great difference in troop strength, the fight was so intense that it led Patterson to overestimate the Confederate troops tenfold. As the Confederates retreated, Patterson backed off as well. This allowed Jackson and his brigade to continue on to Manassas to reinforce Beauregard.

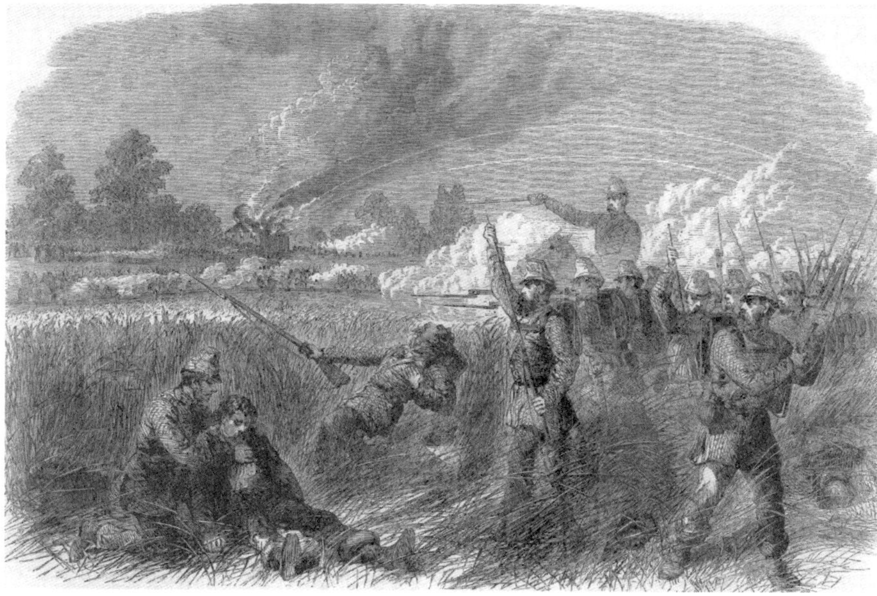

Skirmish at Hainsville, Virginia.

Vizetelly was traveling with the First Wisconsin Infantry, part of Patterson's army. He sketched the Wisconsin men engaging the Confederates at the Porterfield Farm. He reported, "Their [First Wisconsin's] behavior, considering it was the first time they were under fire, was admirable. They went on very steadily, poured in two or three volleys, and then making a rush with bowie-knife and revolver, sent the Disunionists flying towards Winchester, leaving behind many dead, wounded, and prisoners."

Actually, the Confederate losses were small. In his sketch, the First Wisconsin is in a wheatfield firing on Confederates at the tree line and behind a fence. The mounted officer in the illustration is the commander, Colonel Starkweather.

The skirmish at Hainsville, also known as the Battle of Hoke's Run or the Battle of Falling Waters, was the first battle in the Shenandoah Valley. At the time, no one, including Vizetelly, could appreciate the significance of this small skirmish, but Patterson's inability to tie up Johnston's army in the valley would have a big impact at Manassas Junction three weeks later.

After the Hainsville skirmish, Vizetelly traveled to Fairfax, where he witnessed General McDowell's march out of Washington. At Fairfax he sketched a group of Confederate pickets from South Carolina retreating on

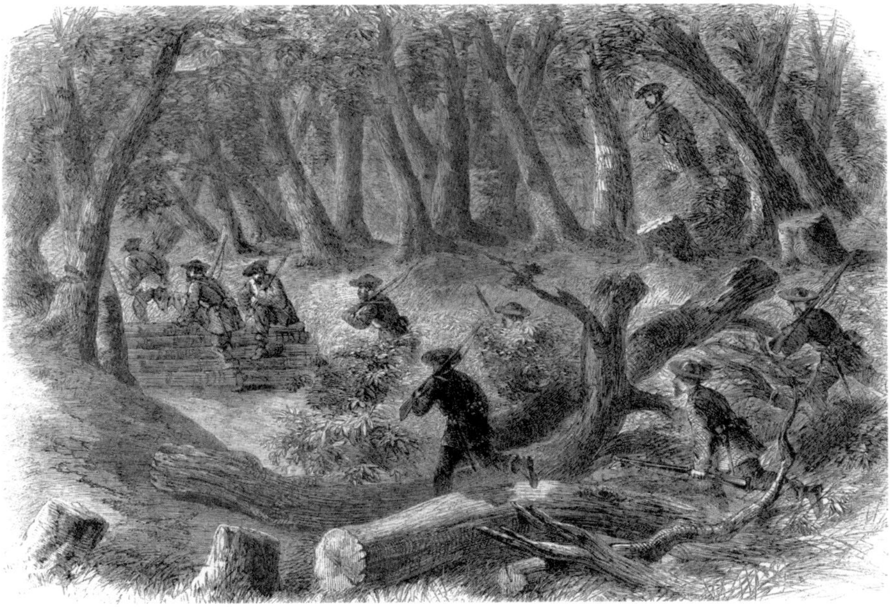

Confederate pickets retreating on the advance of Federal troops.

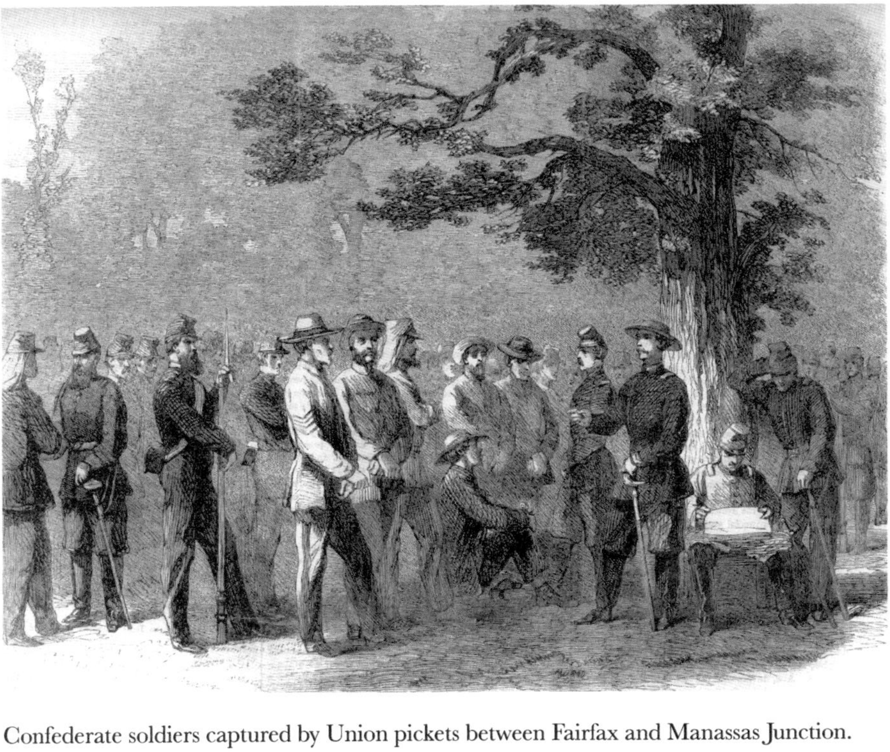

Confederate soldiers captured by Union pickets between Fairfax and Manassas Junction.

seeing McDowell's force and a group of prisoners captured by the Union pickets between Fairfax and Manassas.

As McDowell marched out of Washington on July 16 with thirty-five thousand men, his plan was to advance in three columns and, upon reaching the Confederates at Manassas Junction, flank the enemy on the right, sweeping behind them to cut the railroad to Richmond and threaten the rear of the Confederate force. He was convinced that this would force the Confederate army to drop back to the Rappahannock River.

Manassas was a railroad junction, twenty-five miles from Washington. Bull's Run is a stream that intersects the railway running from Alexandria to Manassas. The stream runs through a group of hills and gorges with steep wooded banks. During the Civil War, the South typically named battles for the name of the town or region where it was fought, in this case the Battle of Manassas. The North sometimes named a battle for a specific geographic feature like a stream or river—in this case the Battle of Bull Run.

While the Federal army was advancing, General Joe Johnston had taken his army to Piedmont Station in the Shenandoah Valley and transported them by rail to join Beauregard at Manassas.

On Thursday, July 18, when the Federal scouts reached Centreville, just four miles out from the Confederate position, it was determined that the route to flank the Confederates on their right was impractical. The roads were narrow and crooked, leaving it impossible to bring up the needed artillery to support the infantry move.

The Union army paused on Friday while another plan of attack could be devised. Even though the route was long and circuitous, McDowell decided to attack Beauregard's left flank on the northern side.

Saturday was devoted to bring the full Federal force up close to Centreville to be positioned for a Sunday morning attack. On the northern flank, the road from Centreville led through a forest and then through a succession of rolling knolls for a quarter of a mile leading to a stone bridge. After the bridge, the road ascended up a steady slope. At the top of the slope Beauregard placed several heavy batteries.

Union gunnery officer Peter Conover Hains had the responsibility of firing the first gun, a thirty-pound Parrott gun, to signal the beginning of the battle. Hains later wrote of the experience:

Three shots at daylight will be the signal for the fight to begin...and as my giant gun was the loudest speaker of the whole armies it was chosen...I would open the fight between the armies of the North and the South.

At a little after six o'clock on as peaceful-appearing a Sabbath morning as that countryside ever knew, the order came. I sighted the rifle carefully, and the men grinned their delight. Then I stood back. "Fire!"...I followed that shot with two others, and the signal had been given to McDowell's army that they were to begin hostilities. The first big battle of the Civil War had begun.

The Confederate batteries did not immediately respond. It was clear that they were awaiting the Federal advance. Just after 11:00 a.m., the First Ohio and Second New York were ordered to advance. When they did so, a Confederate battery opened up with a relentless fire, finally causing the Union infantry to withdraw. Union batteries were then repositioned to respond by silencing the Confederate guns. By 11:30 a.m., Union regiments from New York, Connecticut and Wisconsin were advancing and pushing the Confederates back.

Vizetelly sketched the Twenty-seventh and Fourteenth New York regiments engaging the Confederates and reported:

About midday the battle raged at its highest. Two of the more gallant charges that I witnessed on the portion of the field where I had taken position, with the first-named regiment, form the subject of the accompanying sketch. The battery on the right was a flying one, supported by a strong body of Confederate infantry hid in the ravine and in the thicket at the top of the hill. On the approach of the 27th Regiment they hastily retreated to the crest of the rise behind their battery, after firing a volley; and on the Federalists steadily advancing the guns were also limbered up and withdrawn from their position. The 27th lost 27 killed and 69 wounded out of a force of 900 men. On the right the 14th New York are rushing at an earthwork mounting position-guns, but, owing to the galling fire of the Confederate sharpshooters in the woods and the admirable serving of the pieces in the battery, were forced to retire with severe loss.

Moving to another vantage point, Vizetelly was able to view the Seventy-first New York engage an Alabama regiment.

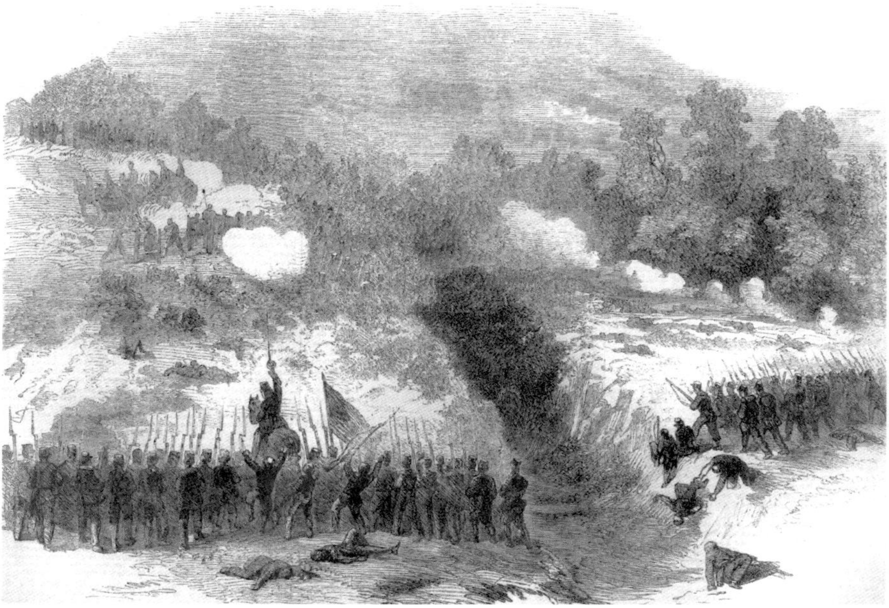

Attack by the Fourteenth and Twenty-seventh New York Regiments at the Battle of Bull Run.

> *This was the only case in which I saw two regiments positively engage each other, and these did no more than blaze away at each other at a distance of three hundred yards until both were badly cut up. The Alabama regiment especially suffered, and when they retired they left the ground covered with their dead and wounded. The 71st lost heavily; but they behaved exceedingly well, loading and firing as if on parade. I think that if the bayonet had been used more freely the matter would have been sooner decided, and with less loss of life. On the hill at the back a Confederate battery was playing on the 71st. I was on the right of the latter regiment.*

Confident of a complete Federal victory, Vizetelly and a correspondent from the London *Times* left the field to go back to Centreville to file their dispatches and sketches and find something to eat.

While the early action did favor the Union army, in the afternoon Jackson's brigade, the Hampton Legion from South Carolina and J.E.B. Stuart's cavalry came up to join the fight. Jackson's battery of thirteen cannons dueled with the Union artillery three hundred yards apart. The Confederate smoothbore guns were much more effective at short range, while the Union "rifled" guns fired many shots over the head of their intended targets.

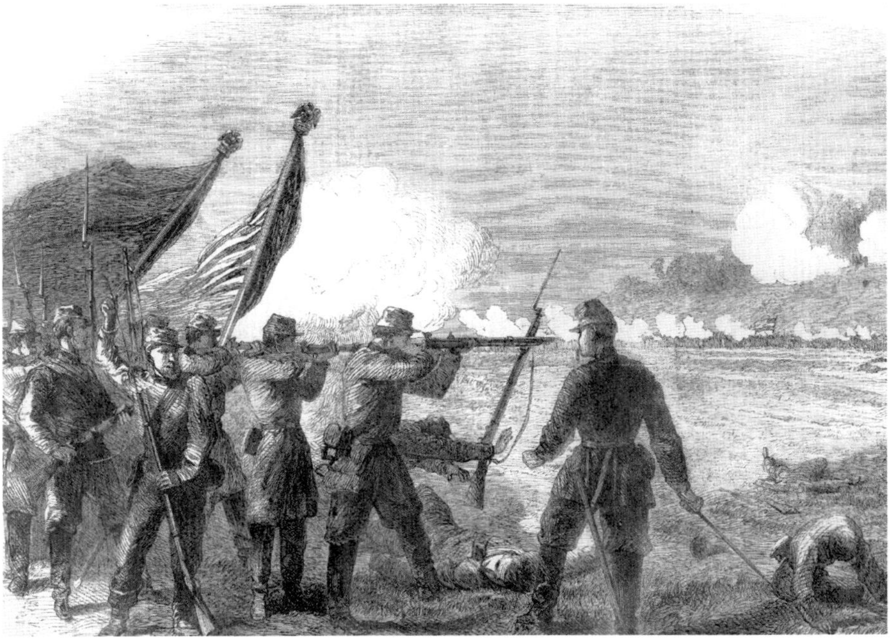

Engagement between the Seventy-first New York and an Alabama regiment at Bull Run.

Forever entrenched in Civil War lore is a reported exchange between South Carolina general Barnard Bee and Colonel Thomas Jackson. As the Union army was still successfully advancing, Bee shouted, "The Enemy are driving us." To which Jackson replied, "Then, Sir, we will give them the bayonet" and refused to leave the field. Reportedly inspired by Jackson's resilience, Bee shouted to his men, "There is Jackson standing like a stone wall. Let us determine to die here, and we will conquer. Follow me!"

The tide of the battle did turn. At 3:00 p.m., the Thirty-third Virginia overran the Federal battery. The Thirty-third's uniforms were blue, causing the Federal artillery gunners to mistake them for Union troops and not fire upon them. The Thirty-third Virginia, joined by Stuart's cavalry, then flanked the Eleventh New York Volunteers (Ellsworth's Fire Zouaves) and scattered the unit. Jackson ordered his men to take a second Union battery, which they did so successfully. With the Union guns then turned on their own men, the tide of the battle turned quickly. By 4:00 p.m., the Union army was repulsed from Henry House Hill, the epicenter of the battle. Beauregard ordered his entire line forward. Initially, the Federal retreat was orderly, but it developed into a rout.

As Vizetelly and his colleague enjoyed their sandwiches in the shade of some trees, a Union officer rode up, announcing, "We've whipped them on all points. We've taken their batteries, and they're all retreating." This news was met with shouts and cheers by all nearby.

Shortly, Vizetelly mounted his horse to return to the field for more sketches. At a bridge he was met by a stream of vehicles in wild disarray. Men were shouting at him, "Retreat…turn back!" Vizetelly and his New York colleague managed to stop an officer running by on foot. "Pray what is the matter sir?" they asked. He shouted, "We're pretty badly whipped!" and continued on.

The London correspondent wrote:

> *Soon I met soldiers who were coming through the corn, mostly without arms; and I presently saw firelocks, cooking-tins, knapsacks, and great-coats on the ground, and observed that the confusion and speed of the baggage carts became greater, and that many of them were crowded with men, or were followed by others who clung to them. The ambulances were crowded with soldiers, but it did not look as if there were many wounded. Negro servants on led horses dashed frantically past; men in uniform whom it were a disgrace to the profession of arms to call "soldiers" swarmed by on mules, chargers, and even draught horses, which had been cut out of carts or wagons, and went on with harness clinging to their heels, as frightened as their riders. Men literally screamed with rage and fright when their way was blocked up.*

Vizetelly, of course, sketched and reported the retreat writing:

> *At half-past five the Federal troops were in full retreat, pursued at different points by the black horse cavalry of Virginia. Retreat is a weak term to use when speaking of this disgraceful rout, for which there was no excuse. The terror-stricken soldiers threw away their arms and accoutrements, herding along like a panic-stricken flock of sheep, with no order whatever in their flight. Those who had been fortunate enough to get places in the baggage-waggons thrust back others with their bayonets and musket-stocks. Wounded men were crushed under the wheels of the heavy, lumbering chariots that dashed down the road at full speed. Light buggies, containing members of Congress, were overturned or dashed to pieces in the horrible confusion of the panic.*

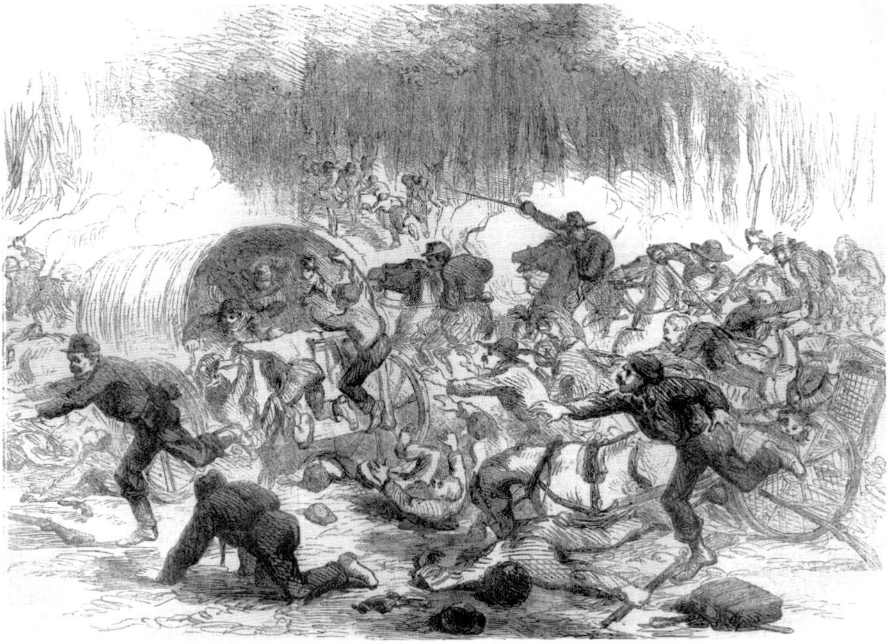

Stampede from Bull Run.

Much of Washington's elite had turned out with picnic baskets and champagne to view the battle and bask in the first Union victory. By day's end, though, the road to Washington was filled with panic-stricken congressmen and civilians.

Union casualties totaled 2,896 compared to 1,982 for the Confederates. However, the Confederates did lose two brigade commanders: Colonel Francis S. Bartow from Georgia and General Barnard Bee from South Carolina, who was mortally wounded and died on July 22.

Northern attorney and diarist George Templeton Strong wrote the day after the battle, "Today will be known as BLACK MONDAY. We are utterly and disgracefully routed, beaten, whipped by secessionists." On that same Monday, Lincoln signed a bill calling for the enlistment of 500,000 men for up to a three-year enlistment. The confident boasting in the North of a quick end to the war was over. When news of the Confederate victory reached Europe, many foreign governments began expressing doubts about the Union's ability to win the war.

The immediate fear in Washington was that the Confederate army, bolstered by this decisive victory, might march on to Washington much like the Federal army had intended to march on Richmond. Professor Thaddeus

S.C. Lowe was charged with performing an aerial reconnaissance with his observation balloon *Enterprise*. Ascending to gauge the Confederate movements, he did not observe any such mass action, much to the relief of the civilian and military authorities in Washington.

President Lincoln summoned General George B. McClellan from West Virginia, appointed him as commander of the military division of the Potomac and charged him with the defense of Washington. General McDowell became the scapegoat for the defeat. General Patterson, who had failed to tie up Johnston in the Shenandoah Valley, was removed from command, given an honorable discharge and mustered out of the army.

Confederate general Beauregard was hailed as a hero in the South. After commanding the firing on Fort Sumter in April and now the great victory at Manassas Junction, he was suddenly one of the most admired men of the new Confederate army. CSA president Jefferson Davis promoted Beauregard from brigadier general to full general.

Vizetelly returned to Washington after the battle to take measure of where to best focus his time. Upon his return to the capital, he sketched a group of Confederate prisoners taken at Bull Run prior to the rout being parading through the streets of the city. He reported:

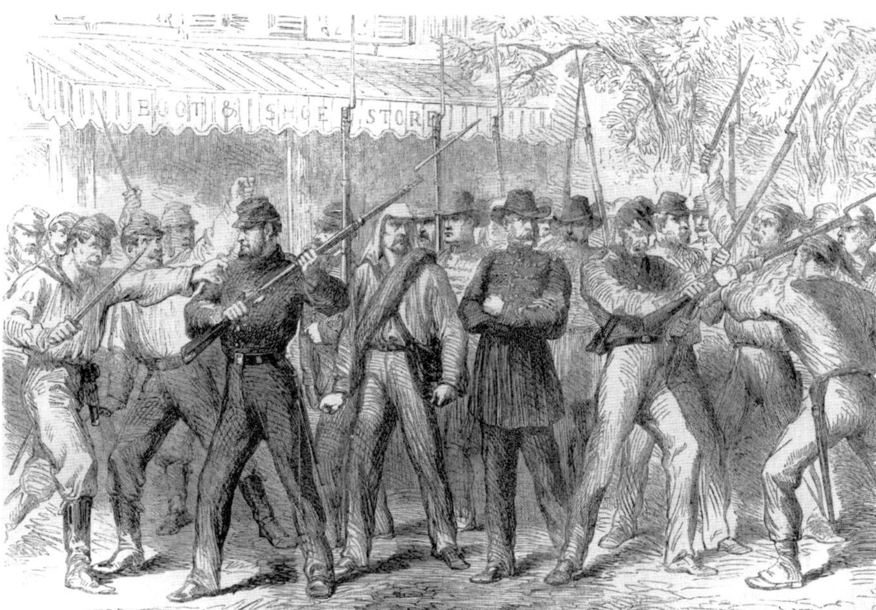

Union troops attacking Confederate prisoners in the streets of Washington.

There was a general impression among the disorganized Federalist soldiers after the battle of Bull Run that their wounded had been inhumanly treated by the Confederates. Many cases of cruelty were narrated, with much circumstantially, in the Unionist journals. Some of them, it is to be feared, were but too true. Among the first to feel the consequences of the anger aroused by the recital of these deeds of cold-blooded cruelty were some wretched prisoners paraded through Pennsylvania Avenue, Washington, two days after the engagement. It was with the greatest difficulty their guard defended them from attacks of the demoralized Union men.

Chapter 4

Deception and Blunders

Life in Washington and Northern Virginia quickly returned to a pace not unlike that prior to the Battle of Manassas. Union troops and politicians were reorganizing and debating in Washington, watching and waiting for the Confederates to move. The Confederates in Northern Virginia were watching and measuring Union troop movements, alerted to a repeat attempt to march on Richmond.

Vizetelly closely monitored the situation as well, anxious to travel with and report on any definitive movement by the Union army. August 1861 was uneventful for Vizetelly and the two armies. By early September, the Union army began stepping up its reconnaissance missions.

One such mission took place on the morning of September 11. A Union regiment led by Brigadier General William F. Smith left Washington by the Chain Bridge and conducted a reconnaissance mission to Lewinsville, Virginia, eleven miles away. Finding no Confederate soldiers present, Smith occupied the town and was later reinforced by a brigade of Union soldiers.

Confederate scouts reported the occupation of Lewinsville to Colonel J.E.B. Stuart who formed men to attack and liberate the town. Stuart's force consisted of 308 Virginia infantry, one artillery company and two companies of light cavalry. Arriving at Lewinsville, Stuart pressed an attack against the Union flank and forced them to retreat from the town.

Vizetelly was present in Washington as the Federal troops wounded at Lewinsville were brought in:

> *Just as the wounded were being brought in, General McClellan reached the ground with an Aide-de-Camp and an escort of dragoons. He raised his hat as each poor fellow was borne from the ambulance to the hospital; and many whose eyes were fast glazing in death raised themselves in the*

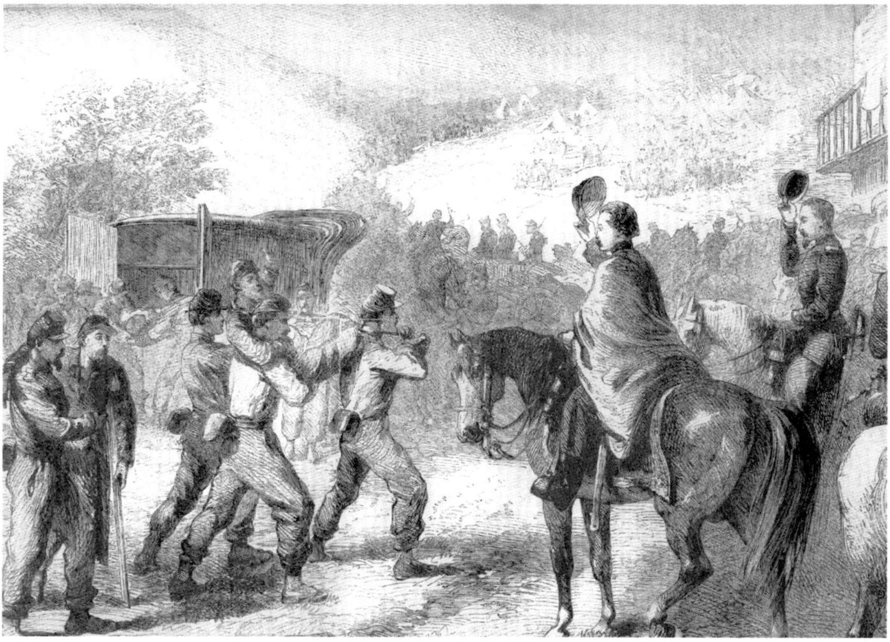

Bringing in the Federal wounded after the skirmish at Lewinsville, Virginia.

> *arms of those who bore them and smiled a last smile at their young and beloved General.*

Vizetelly reported on his own debate as to how best cover the war in America, writing:

> *I expect to go out west to Rosencrantz* [sic] *and Fremont; but yet we may have an attack here from hour to hour, and I dare scarcely leave. Both sides are now awfully close together, and very, very strong. I am waiting to get some definite notion of the next move on the cards, and shall then act promptly.*

However, he could not get a definitive feel for the next significant move by the Union army and chose, therefore, to stay in Washington following Union patrols as they ventured out of the city.

The Confederate camp at Munson's Hill was a great irritant to the Union army. The site was only six miles from Washington and the highest point within ten miles of the Potomac. Munson's Hill afforded a commanding view of the road from Alexandria to Falls Church, the road from Washington to Fairfax, the railroad from Alexandria to Vienna and the intersection at Bailey's Crossroads.

Even from the Chain Bridge at Georgetown, Vizetelly could see an enormous Confederate flag—"the red, white, and blue stripes in which are at least five feet wide each"—at the top of the hill.

Though it was not known initially to Vizetelly and the Union army, the Confederate presence at Munson's Hill was actually a ruse led by J.E.B. Stuart. The site was located between Washington and the Confederate stronghold at Falls Church. Stuart wanted to fool the Union army into believing that his strength at Munson's Hill was substantial.

McClellan had Professor Lowe maintain an aerial reconnaissance with his balloon. Stuart had his troops build faux cannons and, at night, burn multiple large campfires to confuse the enemy.

On September 19, Vizetelly was on patrol with Union pickets when they captured a Confederate deserter:

> *While I was out at the extreme advanced picket in front of the Confederate position at Munson's Hill, I was much startled by a sudden popping all along the enemy's line, the bullets pinging over our heads in every direction. Raising myself cautiously I saw a Confederate soldier bounding through the tall Indian corn, and making for our lines, while two hundred yards behind him his former comrades were doing their best to stop his career. He ran the gauntlet without a single shot taking effect, and turned out to belong to the 13th Virginian Regiment. He told us that Jefferson Davis and Beauregard were on the hill reconnoitering, and that there were 180,000 Confederates between that post and Fairfax.*

In late September, Federal pickets reported that the Confederates had evacuated Munson's Hill. This intelligence was wired to General McClellan, who immediately came out with his staff to join the Union troops marching to occupy the elevated earthwork. Vizetelly fell in with the eight regiments moving to Munson's Hill.

Upon his arrival at Munson's Hill, Vizetelly and the Union regiments were surprised at what they found:

> *A great part of the defenses of the Confederates were make-believe, painted logs for guns and so forth. The scene at the top of the hill in the*

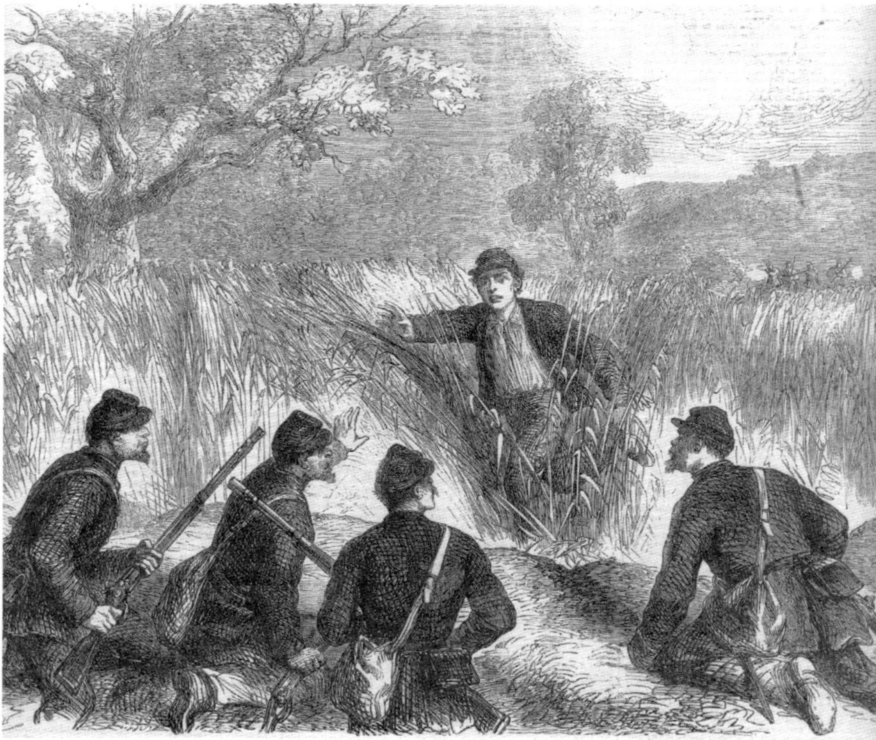

A Confederate deserter coming into the Federal lines at Munson's Hill.

> *earthwork itself, was one of the most amusing that could be imagined. Everybody was laughing. The utter absurdity of the works as a means of defence* [sic], *their smallness, meanness, insignificance, touched everybody's sense of the ludicrous...There are no embrasures for guns, but upon two of its projections are mounted—what? Guns? No, indeed, but old logs, with a black circle painted in the centre of the sawed part to represent a formidable armament.*

Since the Battle of Bull Run, McClellan focused his efforts on building up and training his army for an eventual second march into Virginia and possibly Richmond. On October 19, McClellan ordered Brigadier General George A. McCall to march his division to Dranesville, a small town twelve miles southeast of Leesburg. Intelligence had reported that Confederate colonel Nathan "Shanks" Evans had withdrawn from that position. McCall arrived to find no Confederate soldiers stationed there.

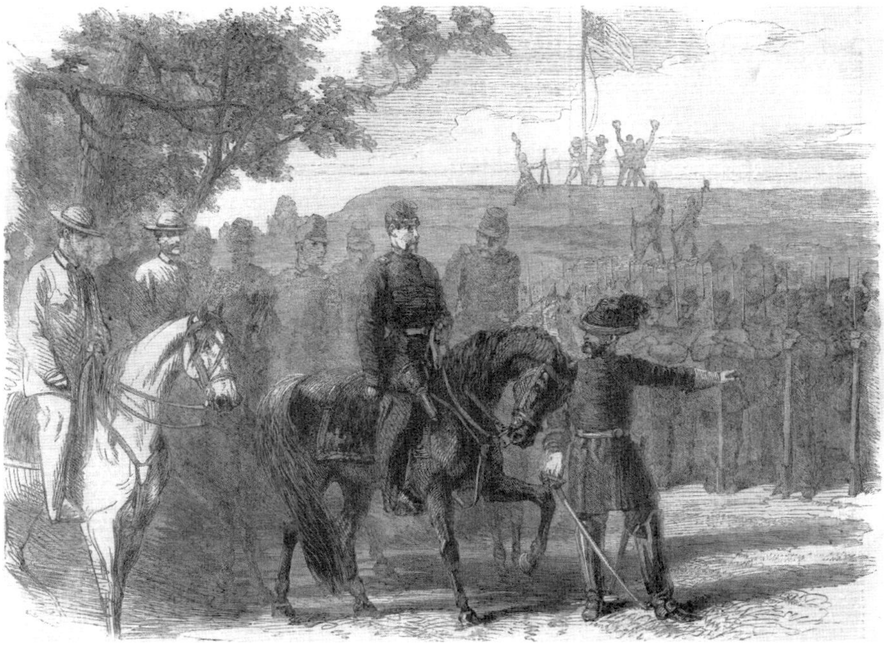

Union general McClellan at Munson's Hill.

A reconnaissance party reported that Evans had taken a defensive position east of town. On October 20, McClellan then ordered Brigadier General Charles Pomeroy Stone to send a raiding party to Evans's position to measure his response. Stone moved his troops to the river at Edwards Ferry and ordered his artillery to fire upon the Confederates. The Confederates did not respond. He then sent a company of men from the First Minnesota across the river and still received no response. A scouting party was sent out at dusk and spotted what they mistakenly thought was a Confederate camp.

At first light, Stone sent the raiding party commanded by Colonel Charles Devens of the Fifteenth Massachusetts Infantry back across the river to attack the reported Confederate camp. They immediately discovered that there was no camp to attack. Devens sent word back to Stone asking for further instructions. Stone sent the remainder of the Fifteenth Massachusetts across the river to join Devens with instructions to move toward Leesburg to conduct a reconnaissance.

Devens encountered the Seventeenth Mississippi Infantry in a skirmish and quickly realized that the Confederates were being reinforced by Evans's troops. Devens withdrew to the river, where he was joined by the remainder of his force. However, there were too few boats to quickly move them back across the river or to reinforce them with Union troops on the other side as the Confederates were continuing to advance.

By 3:00 p.m., an intense fight ensued and continued until dark. The Union troops were driven to the river, where a disorganized retreat caused the death of many Union troops when the few boats were swamped and capsized. Many of the Massachusetts soldiers, including the wounded, drowned trying to cross the river.

With his usual nose for action, Vizetelly was with the Fifteenth Massachusetts when they first crossed the river. He made two sketches of the events and filed this report:

> *The whole affair appears to have been ill-planned, and adds another to the grievous blunders committed by the Federal commanders. It is hardly credible that 1800 men should have been sent across a river in the face of an enemy most strongly posted, and left unsupported when 30,000 of the division to which they belonged were within sound of their rifles. The small body, however, fought gallantly throughout the day against three times their number. One incident in the fight—a desperate effort made by the 15th Massachusetts Regiment to clear the woods by a bayonet charge—is illustrated…This is believed to be the only instance in which a bayonet charge has been attempted by a regiment in the Federal army. The 15th Massachusetts fought most gallantly throughout the whole affair, although they knew the odds were greatly against them; and the example set by their officers, mostly students from Harvard College, Cambridge, was most praiseworthy.*
>
> *Their efforts, however, were not crowned with success, as the deadly fire of the Mississippi riflemen drove them back each time; and, as evening drew on, seeing the utter uselessness of contending against their powerful enemy, the few surviving combatants slowly fell back to the river-side with but two line officers remaining. In the endeavor to re-cross to the island, midway between the Maryland and Virginian shores, from which they had started, the general organization of the force was quite abandoned, each company acting separately. The officers and men who could swim started, half naked, over the river, and the boats were kept awhile for the wounded. This, however, lasted but a little time. All order was quickly lost. A large flat boat was sunk by overcrowding, and scores of men perished, some by drowning and some by the fire of the Confederates, who now*

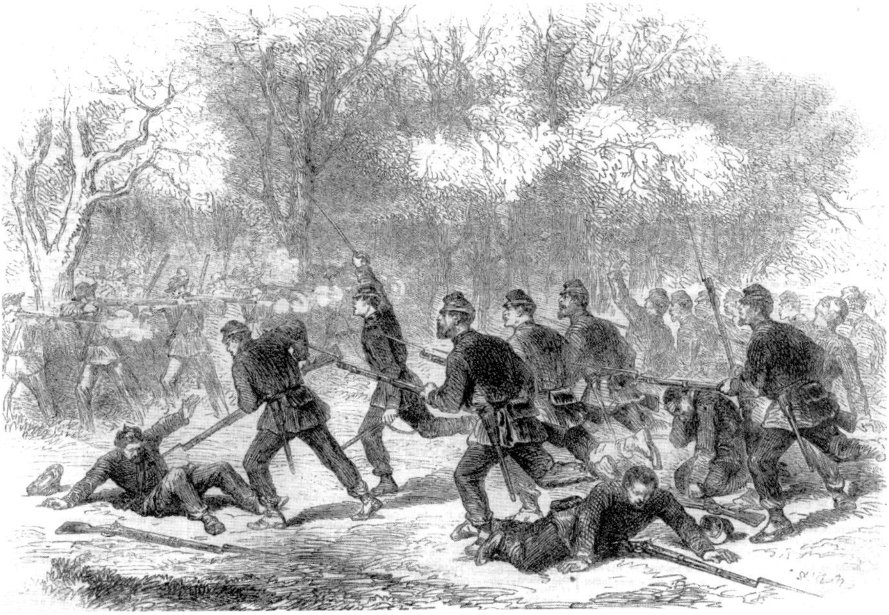

A desperate effort made by the Fifteenth Massachusetts to clear the woods by a bayonet charge at the Battle of Ball's Bluff.

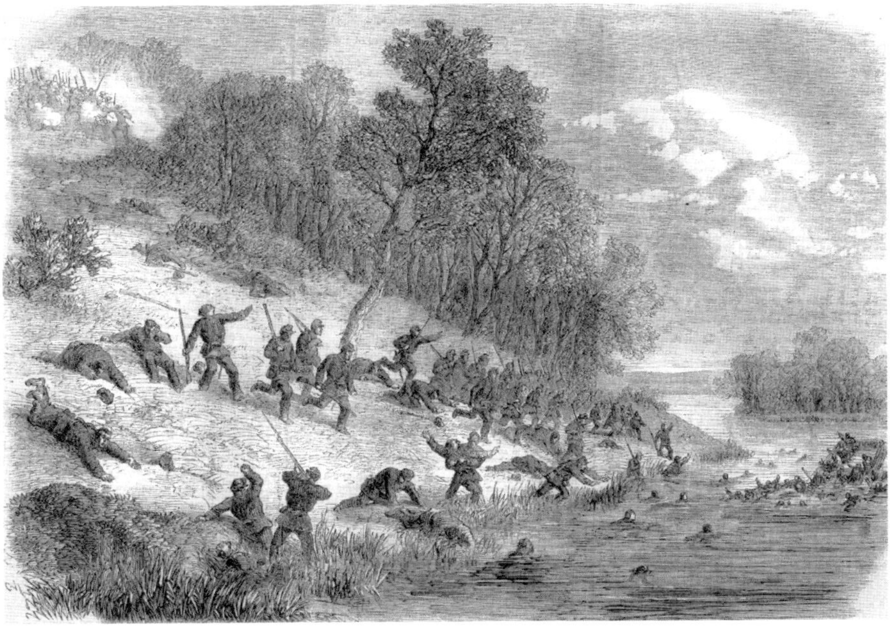

Flight of the Federal troops at the Battle of Ball's Bluff.

> *crowded the high bank and poured an incessant fire upon the scattering fugitives. The river channel was quickly strewed with the dead and dying, but the bearing of the survivors is reported to have been strangely quiet—the immobility, perhaps, of desperate hopelessness. Hundreds, probably, here were sacrificed. This much is certain, that out of the 1800 who landed scarcely 600 returned.*

Vizetelly was mistaken regarding the size of the Confederate force, as both sides placed approximately 1,800 men in action. However, he was more accurate about the Federal casualties, which totaled 1,002 compared to only 155 for the Confederates.

One Union officer killed was Colonel Edward Dickinson Baker, who was also a U.S. senator from Oregon. His death marks the only time that a sitting U.S. senator was killed in battle.

Congress was infuriated over the loss of Senator Baker and the mounting losses in the eastern theatre of the war. Legislation was passed to form the Congressional Joint Committee on the Conduct of the War. This committee led to continuous political infighting and pitted congressmen against career military officers as their military decisions were constantly second-guessed for the remainder of the long war.

Chapter 5

Growing Restless

After Ball's Bluff, there was little activity of any real importance in the eastern theatre. Vizetelly reported:

> *The only persons who appear to me to display any amount of activity are the greedy hordes of hungry contractors, who are determined to have their pound of flesh from the sorely pressed Union…I'm getting tired of this continual "wait another week and you will see something done" which I am constantly being told by officers in high command.*

While little else to do, Vizetelly turned to illustrating camp life.

At times the routine and monotony of camp life was interrupted by most unpleasant necessities. Such was the case when Vizetelly witnessed the sentence being carried out for a Union soldier convicted of desertion. A young private in the Lincoln Cavalry was convicted and sentenced to death by firing squad at the camp at Fairfax Seminary. The soldier was given his last rites by a Roman Catholic priest in camp. He was then set on his own coffin as a squad of eight men passed sentence.

Vizetelly sometimes chose to forego the night amusements in camp to stand with the pickets on the Potomac River. He reported:

> *Frequently there are alarms in the Federal camp on the Potomac at night caused by the driving in of our pickets and the appearance in force of the Confederates at different points of the Union lines. On these occasions it is necessary to communicate with the Commander-in-Chief, and to do this expeditiously a new system of signals has been introduced into the Federal army. By day messages are sent from one division to another by use of differently coloured flags, thus doing away with the necessity of dispatching*

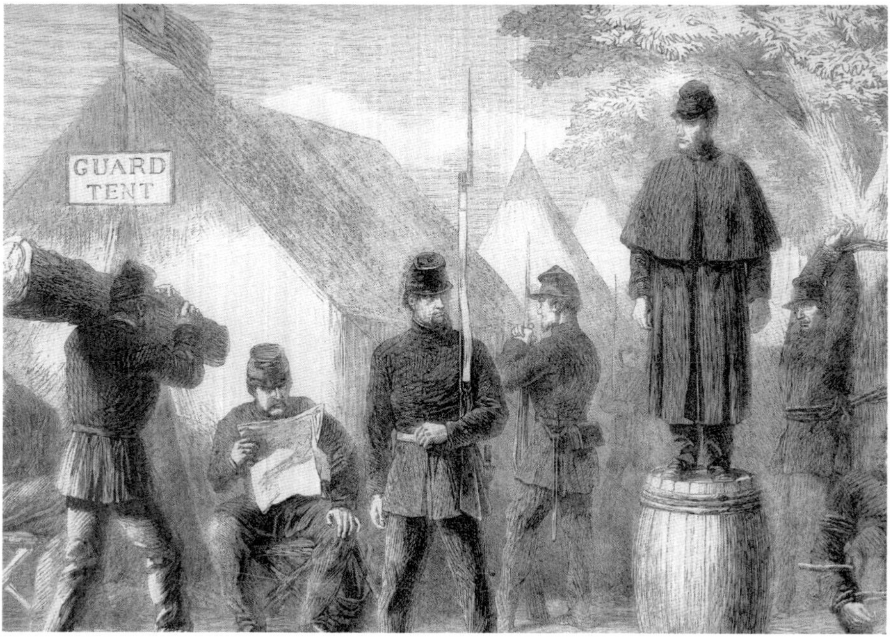

Punishment drill in the Federal camp.

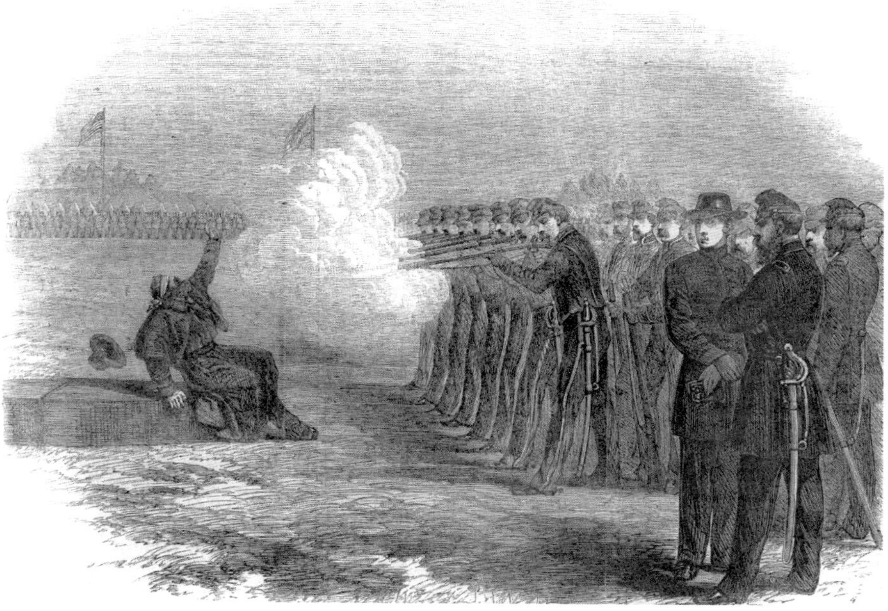

Execution of a deserter in the Federal camp at Fairfax Seminary.

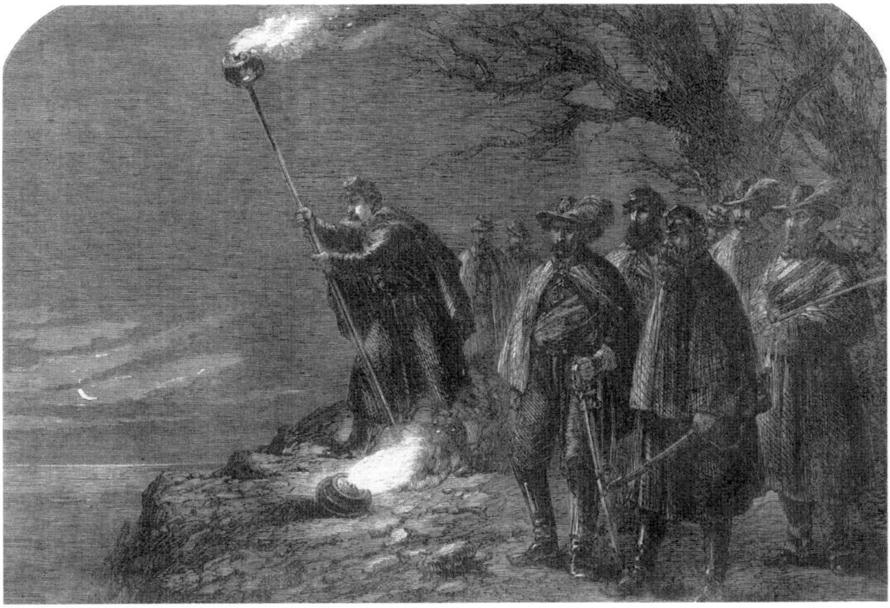

Signaling to Washington from the banks of the Potomac.

> *mounted troopers with written orders; and by night lamp-torches take their place with the same effect. These signals can be used with an army in motion, the corps attached to the different brigades occupying as they move all elevations or lofty buildings on their route. At the signalman's feet lies a large brass lamp, which is the axis around which the motive light forms its curves—each curve, according to the direction which it takes, signifying a number the meaning of which number being known only to the officer commanding each corps.*

In the fall of 1861, England was caught in the crossfire between the newly formed Confederate States and the Federal government, each expecting and, in some cases, demanding the public support of the Crown. Vizetelly noted in one report "an irritability among the more sensitive spirits of the Federal states against England on account of the decided principle of non-intervention." An editorial in the *Illustrated London News* recognized "the Confederates believe that, in our secret hearts, our leaning is to their side, and that our sympathies are, so to speak, wrapped up in cotton…We have waited in vain up to the moment at which we are writing for the decision of her majesty's government on this subject."

In October, England's neutrality was threatened by an action of the United States Navy in a case that drew international attention. In October 1861, President Jefferson Davis appointed John Slidell and James M. Mason as diplomatic commissioners to represent the Confederate States to negotiate treaties with England and France. Their principal task was to secure recognition of the Confederate States as a nation.

Slidell and Mason departed by running the Union blockade aboard the swift *Theodora* bound for Havana, Cuba. In Havana they booked passage aboard the British merchant ship *Trent.* Captain Charles Wilkes of the USS *San Jacinto* was patrolling off Havana with the intent of seizing Slidell and Mason to prevent their reaching Europe.

When Wilkes spotted the *Trent* leaving port, he ordered the command to "beat to quarters, hoist the colors and load the guns." Wilkes fired a shot across the bow of the unarmed British ship, but Captain Moir commanding the *Trent* displayed the British colors and did not stop. Wilkes then fired a second shot directly across the path of the *Trent.* This time Moir had no choice but to relent.

An armed party led by the executive officer Lieutenant Fairfax boarded the *Trent* and demanded the passenger list. Captain Moir protested this armed invasion as a breach of international law and refused to present any papers or the Confederate commissioners. After additional armed marines arrived, Slidell, Mason and their two associates presented themselves to Lieutenant Fairfax, who forcibly transferred them to the *San Jacinto.* With the mission accomplished, the *Trent* was allowed to continue, and the *San Jacinto* sailed to Fortress Monroe with their prisoners.

The armed seizure of a British ship quickly became the subject of much debate across the world and incited tensions between the United States and England. The *Illustrated London News* covered the controversy with stories and illustrations of the two ships and all the major parties involved. In an editorial, the paper noted, "The British public has been agitated by intense excitement during the past week by the apparent imminence of a rupture of friendly relations between this country and America."

With little military action in the field, Vizetelly turned his attention to the public discussions of the maritime legal case being pressed by England. The British government demanded an apology and the return of the four Confederates diplomats to England. Vizetelly reported, "In the discussions that have been created by this all-absorbing topic of Slidell and Mason, much has been elicited that is antagonistic to England."

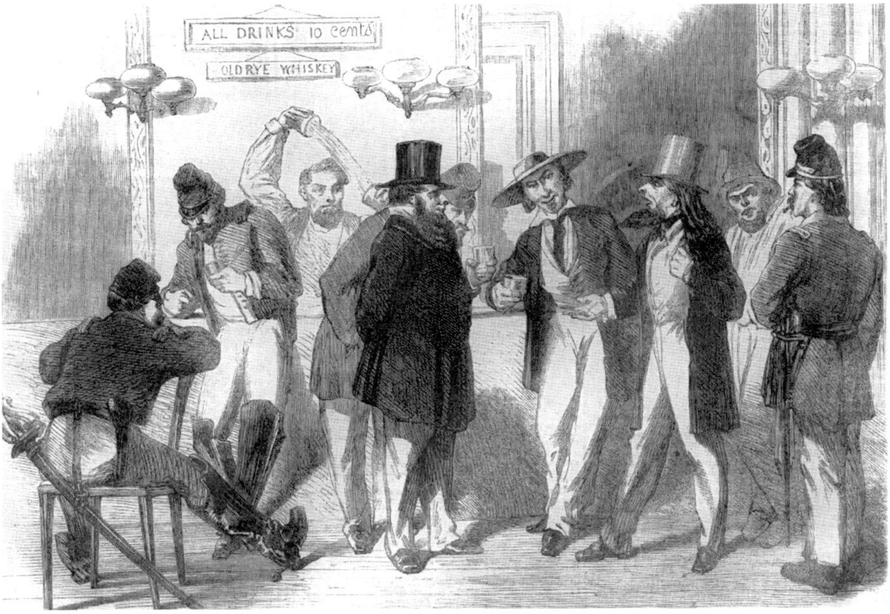

The Slidell and Mason case argued at a Washington bar.

After more than a month of intense negotiations, U.S. secretary of state William Seward made an official apology to the British government, writing that "the four persons in question are now held in military custody at Fort Warren in the State of Massachusetts. They will be cheerfully liberated. Your Lordship will please indicate a time and place for receiving them." Much to the disappointment of the Confederate government, once the case was resolved, the controversy between the United States and England quickly disappeared from the news.

There still were several skirmishes that Vizetelly did cover for the newspaper. With little real military action in the eastern theatre, Vizetelly's ability to be in the right place at the right time continued to serve him well:

> *During my visit a dozen or so of small schooners of light draught successfully ran the blockade by hugging the Maryland shore closely, where the water shoals considerably. Heavy ships dare not risk it... We on our side watched the little ships anxiously as they came within range of the enemy's guns, which they no sooner did than a terrible fire of shot and shell opened upon them, not one, however, being struck seriously, and all enabled to keep their river down the river. We, the spectators, ran probably more risk than*

the vessels, for many of the shells came over to our neighborhood, bursting in close proximity to where we stood. Our turn then came and we gave them a few rounds from the tiny Parrots, pitching the 10-pound shells right into their works, peppering a steamer, one of the Confederate navy, until they were glad to have her inside Quantico Creek...My "Reconnaissance with General Sickles in the Bed of the Potomac" was a most remarkable ride, for nearly the whole time we had to wade our horses' girths in the river

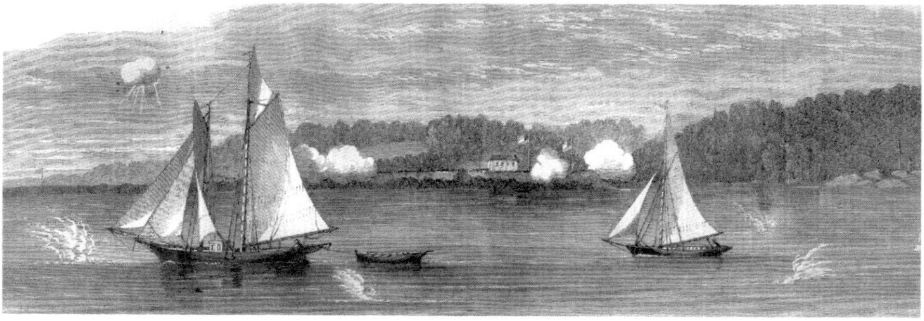

Federal supply schooners running the Confederate blockade at Ball's Ferry.

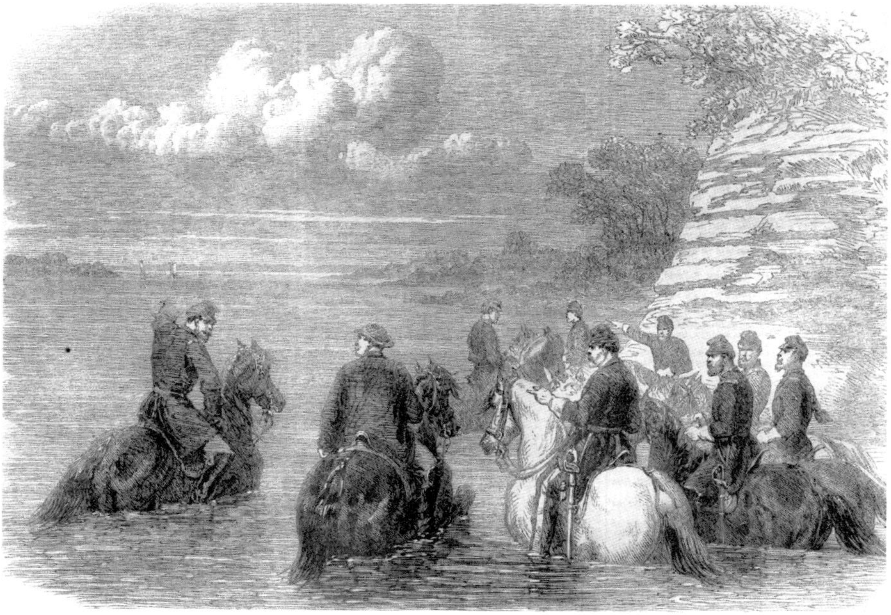

Vizetelly on reconnaissance with Union general Sickles on the Potomac.

itself, sometimes even swimming, the banks being impractical in places—the neighborhood is Indian Head, close by the batteries.

Two weeks later, Vizetelly was riding with the Fourteenth New York Regiment near Falls Church when they were attacked by Confederate cavalry. The raiding party carried off thirty-six prisoners and six wagons of supplies before the Brooklyn unit could fall back.

Once again, while patrolling with an advance guard of General Blenker's division at Annandale, Virginia, he was surprised by a raid by Confederate cavalry:

We were attacked by a squadron of Confederate cavalry—fine, rough looking fellows, dressed in non-descript uniforms, red shirts, gray tunics; some with boots and some without; armed with sabers and revolvers. Many of them were very powerfully built, and as they rushed in among the men of the 45th New York, they clutched at them and dragged off 13 at a gallop.

Other than the occasional skirmish, by late 1861, there was little of interest to illustrate. Sketches of Washington events and camp life were

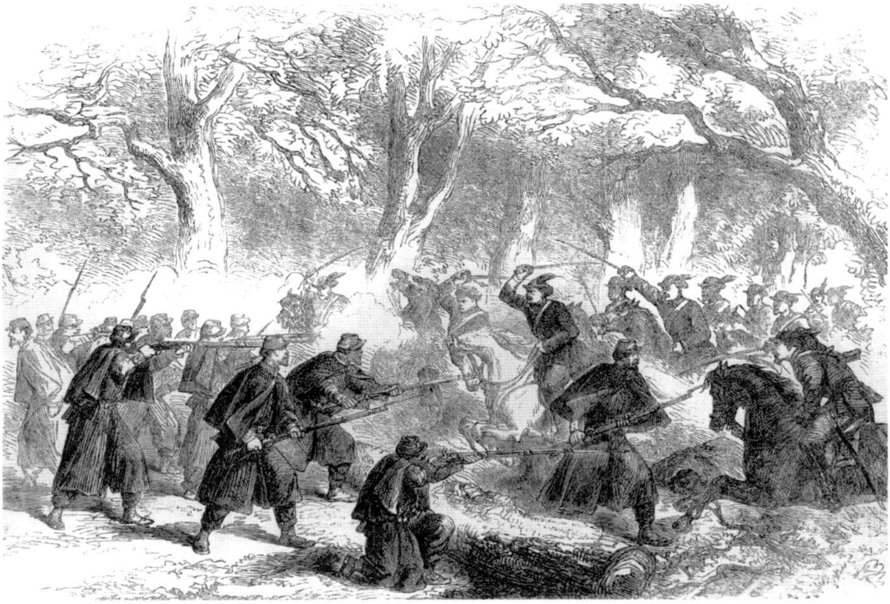

Skirmish between the Fourteenth New York Regiment from Brooklyn and Confederate cavalry at Falls Church.

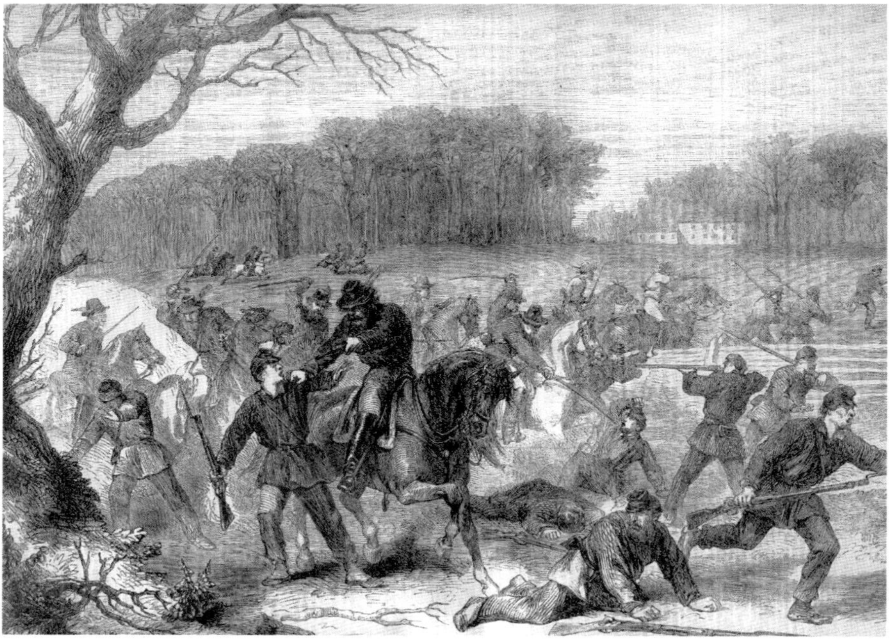

Advanced post of General Blenker's division surprised by Confederate cavalry at Annandale, Virginia.

being crowded out by illustrations of the death and funeral of His Royal Highness the Prince Consort, the husband of Queen Victoria.

One illustration that did get published was a New Year's Day reception at the White House. Vizetelly reported:

> *Well, as diplomatic relations had not broken off between the Court of St. James's and the White House, I assisted to swell the crowd of anything but swells who went to pay their respects to the President on New-Year's Day. The diplomatic corps were first in making the morning call de rigueur; then followed the officers of the army and navy; and the mobility, with whom I was, came last, getting but a feeble shake from the exhausted Presidential hand and arm…The lion of the reception was Judge Harney, from the territory of New Mexico, who appeared in full hunting costume of deerskin, attracting everyone's attention by his picturesque ensemble…*
>
> *The visitors pass directly in front of the Chief of the State, and each appears…the endeavor to squeeze the nails out of the president's fingers,*

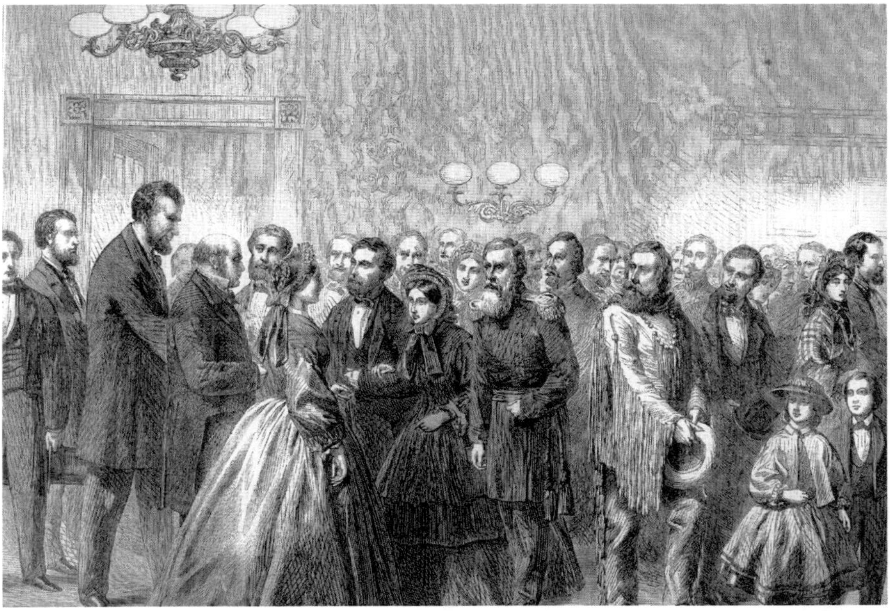

New Year's Day reception at the White House.

who, by-the-by, appears to have a pleasant word for everybody, and especially addresses himself to the ladies and children.

New Year's Day is celebrated with great enthusiasm by the Americans generally. The custom which requires the ladies of a family to keep open house for all gentlemen who choose to call grew up in New York, which city is said to have imported it from Amsterdam, the mother city.

Chapter 6

Burnside's Expedition

Through his extensive network of diplomatic and military contacts, Vizetelly learned that General Ambrose Burnside was to lead an offensive expedition to "some unknown point in Dixie." He promptly applied for a permit to accompany the expedition, which was granted on January 10. When the ships departed, the destination was still unknown, but rumors abounded to include destinations as far away as Galveston, Texas.

Vizetelly was assigned to the *Picket*, a small steamer that would transport Burnside and his senior staff. The Englishman found himself assigned to a small six-foot cabin with five other men. Burnside selected the *Picket* because it was thought to be the least seaworthy of the ships in the task force fleet, and he was determined to put none of his men ahead of himself in comfort and safety.

The entourage sailed downstream to Fortress Monroe, where a fleet of more than one hundred transport and supply ships, several river steamers refitted as gunboats and sixteen thousand soldiers were assembled. The fleet departed, the eventual destination known only to Burnside's closest advisors.

Finally, when the fleet reached Cape Henry, everyone aboard the *Picket* was briefed on the mission. The goal was to cut off "communication of the Secessionists on the Potomac with the Southern Seaboard States." Their destination was Roanoke Island, North Carolina, to capture the Confederate position there. If successful, the task force was to proceed to New Berne and on into central North Carolina, destroying the rail lines and telegraph capabilities.

While en route, the task force encountered heavy seas off Cape Hatteras. Vizetelly was almost lost overboard. He wrote:

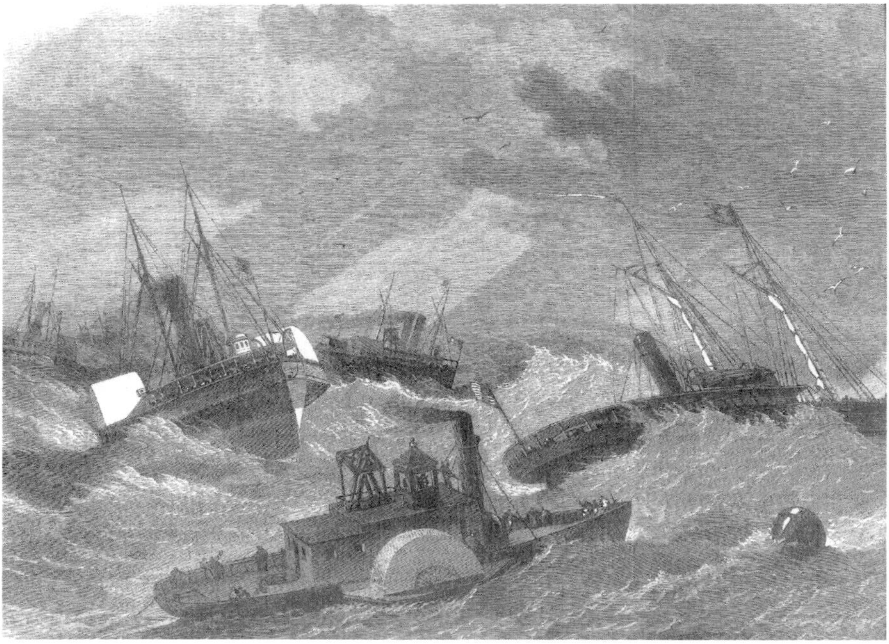

The *Picket* leading the ships of the Burnside Expedition over the Hatteras Bar in North Carolina.

> *For a moment we all thought we were going to "turn turtle," and I, who had just laid down on a couch in the deck-cabin, was hurled against the door, which burst open with the concussion and shot me through it into the lee scuppers, where I rolled about in six or eight inches of the wholesome briny.*

Burnside and his entourage, including Vizetelly, transferred to a larger steamer, the USS *Guide.* Vizetelly noted that the breakers off the Hatteras Bar were sometimes twenty feet high.

The task force later anchored in Pamlico Sound and transferred the troops to land. Vizetelly was not impressed with their quarters, writing, "On this land, partially submerged at high water, are built forts…but to my mind the greatest harm that could have been done the Confederates would have been to leave them quietly in possession of this Godforsaken spot…judge for yourself if such a place is fit for habitation by aught clams and muscles."

On January 14, the day after the arrival of the task force, the steamer *City of New York* became hung up on a sandbar. The intense waves and rough

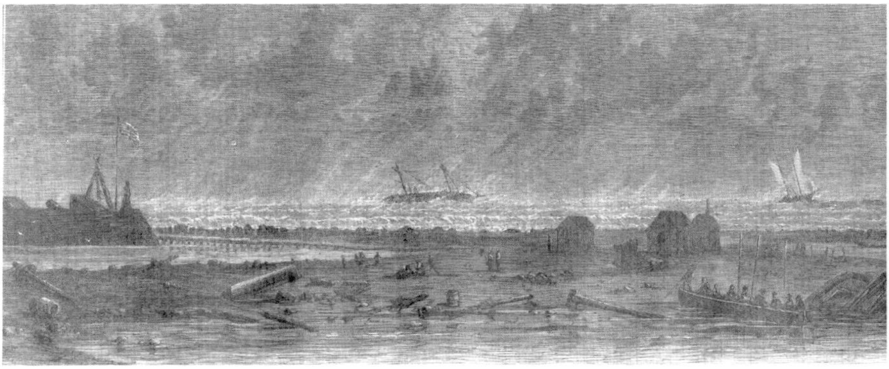

Hatteras Spit, with the wreck of the *City of New York* on the bar in the distance.

current destroyed the ship as it lay aground. Vizetelly observed, "Fortunately, the crew and those on board were saved in surf-boats, but three other poor fellows attempting to reach the harbor in a launch from the weather-bound vessel outside got capsized in the breakers and sank before our eyes."

The rough seas at Hatteras took a toll on the task force, perhaps a more dangerous enemy than the Confederates they would face. By January 15, there were four ships wrecked and six vessels washed ashore. Of particular concern was the loss of the USS *Pocahontas* with ninety horses aboard, of which only twenty-five were saved. Other supply ships that were to follow the task force with provisions never arrived.

On the trip, Vizetelly had ample opportunity to observe the crews and form an opinion as to their competency. Of the crew, he reported:

> *I have been here long enough to ascertain one fact, and that is, with a few exceptions, General Burnside is the only competent man in the expedition; and, from the personal respect and friendship I feel for him, I trust he is not going to be made the scapegoat of the apathy, supineness, and incompetency of others. The Commodore, whose duty it should have been to attend to everything connected with the sea transport of the troops, has shown himself but twice in the quarter-galley of his ship, and each time with his hands thrust deeply into his pockets, gazing listlessly at ships running ashore or drifting into each other. General Burnside, on the contrary, has performed all the duties of a harbor-master, narrowly escaping being swamped on more than one occasion. Whenever a ship has been in distress the General has been the first man off to her assistance; and there is not a grade in his*

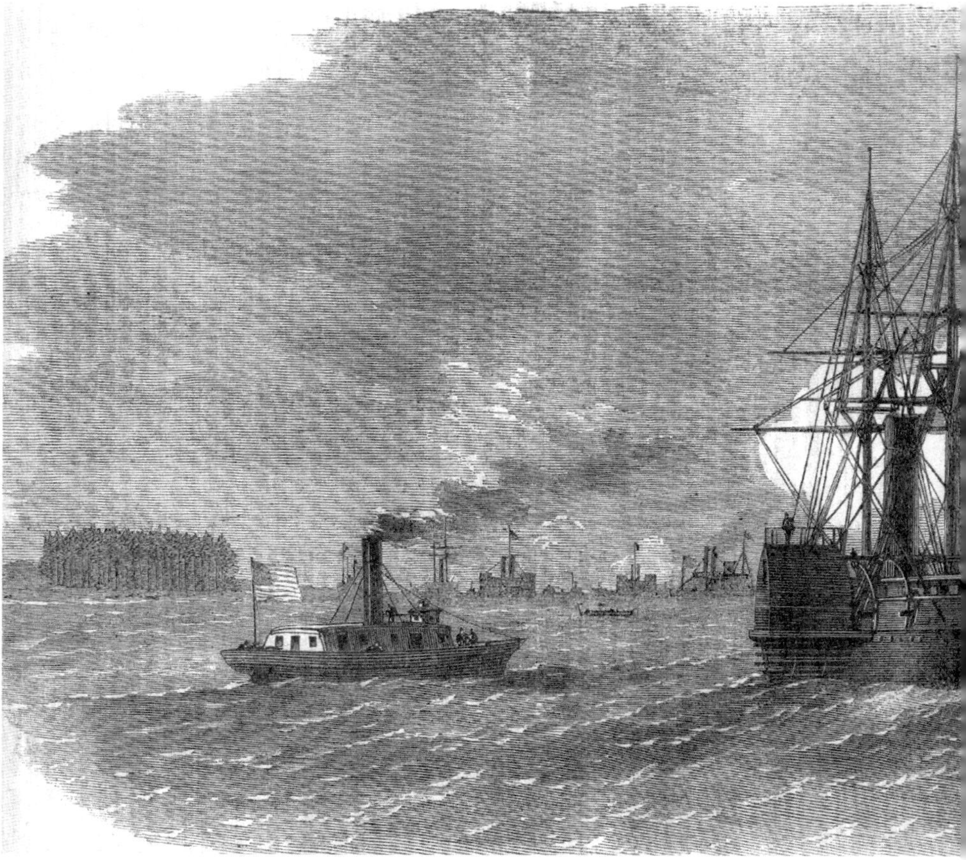

Attack on the Confederate batteries at Roanoke Island by Federal gunboats.

> *army that he has not filled during the last fortnight, so anxious is he for the wellbeing and comfort of his troops.*

Once again, Burnside moved his senior command to another ship, the USS *Spalding*, prior to organizing the first of several attacks. Vizetelly wrote:

> *If we are to believe the contrabands who make their way here hourly, preparations have been made to give us a warm reception. They tell us the Confederates have a dozen gun-boats and some powerful shore batteries mounted with 100-pounders. In our expedition there cannot be less than seventy or eighty guns afloat; so I suppose when the entertainment commences there will be lots of noise made.*

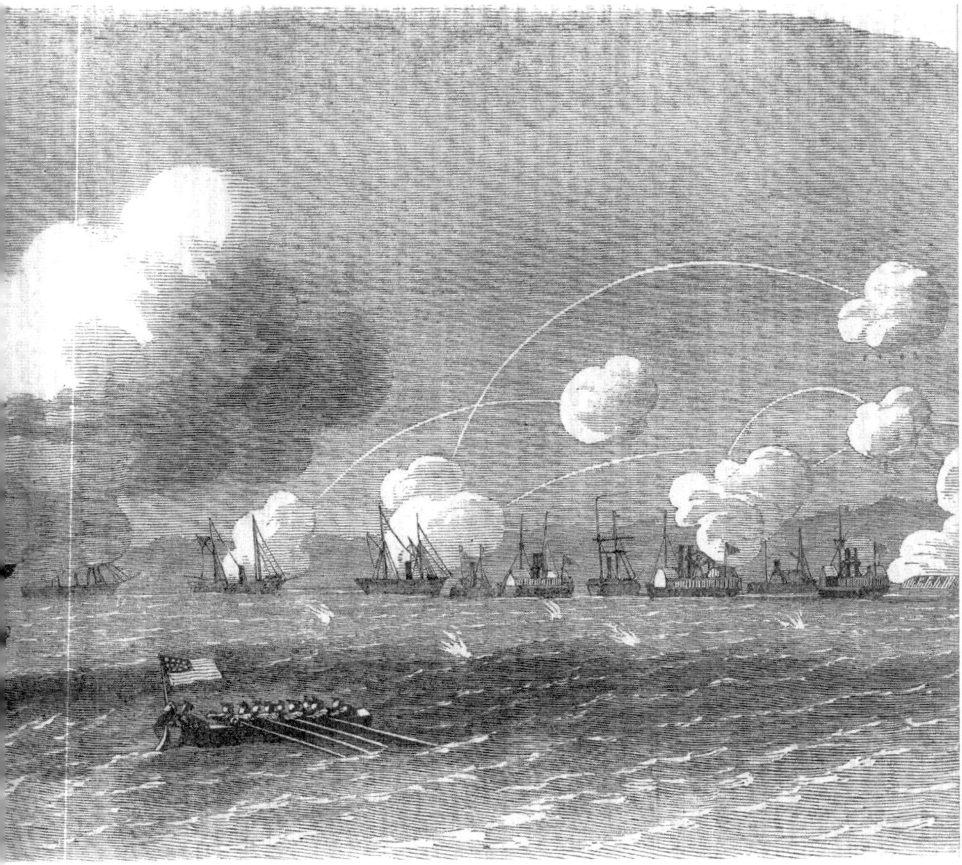

Understanding the geography of the Outer Banks at North Carolina, it was clear that Roanoke Island was the key. In 1861, Confederate forces established a series of small earthwork fortifications on the island. Burnside's task force still had to cross through Hatteras Inlet to get into Pamlico Sound. The commodore thought that he had eight feet of swash to get through the inlet but found he had much less. Some of the ships drew too much water to make it and had to be lightened and pulled through by cables. Some of the ships could not make it through at all and had to leave the task force. It was February 4 before the ships that could make it had crossed Hatteras Inlet.

The next day, the fleet assembled and anchored near the southern end of Roanoke Island. On February 7, the bombardment of Fort Bartow on Pork Point began. Burnside landed his troops by 3:00 p.m., and the defenders at Fort Bartow fled, allowing the position to be taken without opposition.

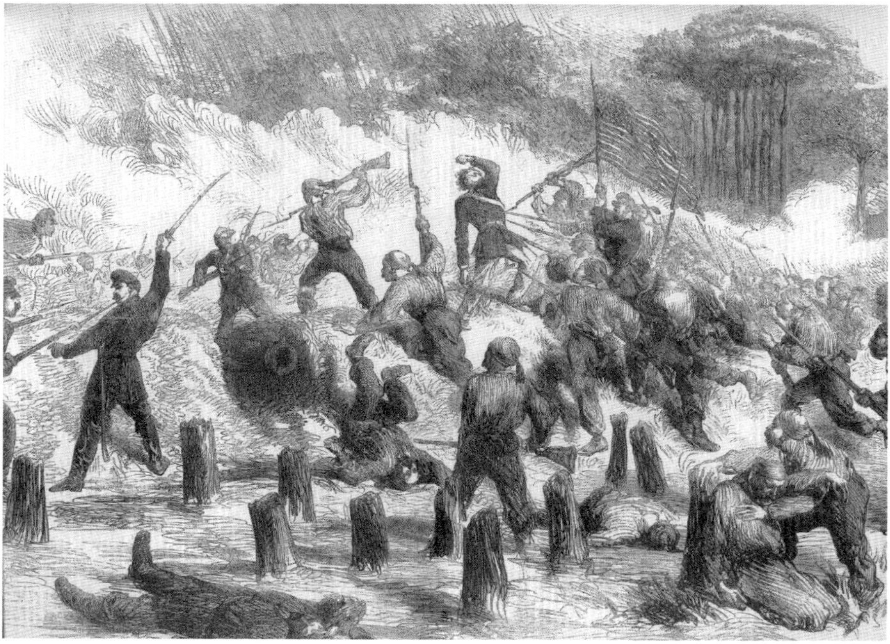

The Ninth New York (Hawkins's Zouaves) and the Twenty-first Massachusetts in a bayonet charge on the Confederate fieldworks.

The next day, Burnside's troops advanced across the interior of the island, meeting light resistance. By day's end, the Federal troops had control of the island and 2,500 Confederate prisoners.

Vizetelly had the opportunity to interview several of the North Carolinians residing on the island:

> *With regard to the sentiment of the people on the island, it appears to me to be quite as much one way as the other. I think all they want is to be let alone by both parties. The following were more especially the sentiments of Mr. Jarvis, farmer and fisherman, whose house had been taken possession of by the Zouaves; he was a perfectly bewildered individual. His family was in one of the Negro shanties, and he was outside, mourning over the events of the day. He had "nothing agin the North," and had sold a great many shad to go there. But the troops had killed one of his pigs, and his wife had lost her temper and her flat irons. "Do you own any negroes, Mr. Jarvis?" queried I, "Well, I did, but three of 'em went to Hatteras last week, two more have run away, I don't know where, and there's one in the kitchen I'll*

> *give away if anybody wants him!" It was a clear case of unmistakable collapse. He was assured by one of the Staff who was present, that his remaining property should be protected, and that all deficiencies should be made good if he was loyal.*

Once on Roanoke Island, Vizetelly picked up on rumors of a pending Federal attack on Manassas, and he made plans to immediately return to Virginia. After his experiences since joining Burnside's expedition, Vizetelly remarked that he was "heartily sick of combined naval and military expeditions, and have thoroughly determined to have nothing more to do with them."

Chapter 7

Heading West

On his return to Virginia, still no major campaign by the Union army materialized. Biding his time, Vizetelly accompanied every scouting and raiding party that would have him. He traveled with the Union army to Centreville in early March as it advanced on Confederate positions in that city. After securing Centreville, Vizetelly accompanied Federal cavalry scouts to Manassas Junction after the evacuation by the Confederates.

Once Manassas Junction was occupied, Vizetelly traveled with a cavalry unit led by General George Stoneman Jr. Stoneman's unit followed the retreating Confederate army for twenty-seven miles. There were two Orleanist Princes, the Comte de Paris and the Duc de Chartres traveling with Stoneman. At Cedar Run, Stoneman's unit interviewed escaped slaves to gather intelligence about the next Confederate stronghold at Gordonsville.

Returning to Washington, Vizetelly was anxious to join General George McClellan as he planned a large troop movement from Washington to southeast Virginia. The plan was to avoid the large concentration of Confederate troops in Northern Virginia by sailing to Yorktown and moving up the York River to advance on Richmond.

With the help of the Comte de Paris, Vizetelly, Sir William Howard Russell of the London *Times*, Lieutenant Colonel Henry Charles Fletcher of the Scots Fusilier Guards and Colonels Rowan and Neville of the British Royal Artillery were issued official passes by the Federal chief of staff to accompany McClellan. Secretary of War Edwin Stanton learned of the foreign entourage and revoked the permits for Vizetelly and Russell—he was still angry over the reports filed by the two British correspondents after the Battle of Manassas, particularly Vizetelly's sketch of the fleeing Union troops.

When McClellan departed Alexandria on March 17, Vizetelly and Russell were angry at being left behind. Russell immediately left for England in a

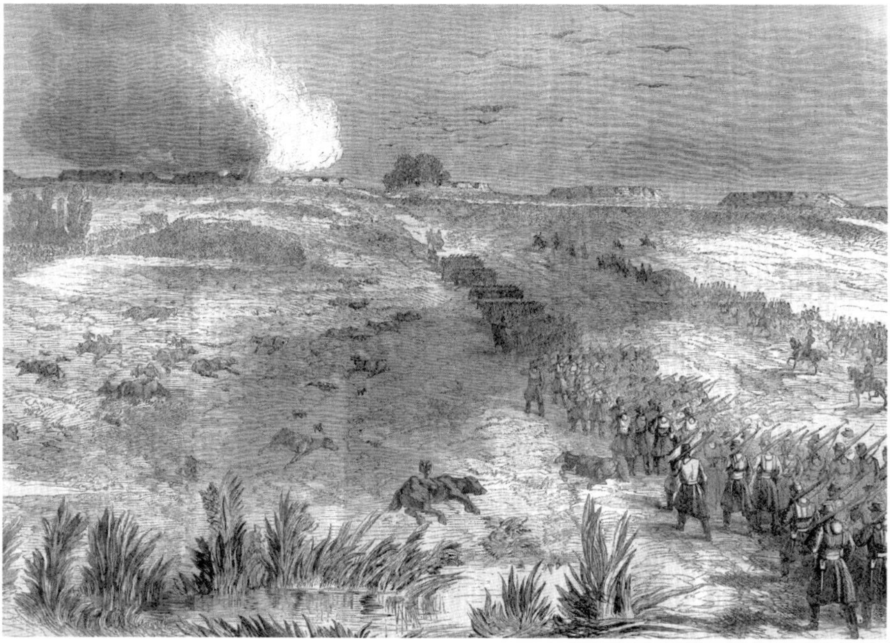

Federal troops advancing on the abandoned Confederate position at Centreville.

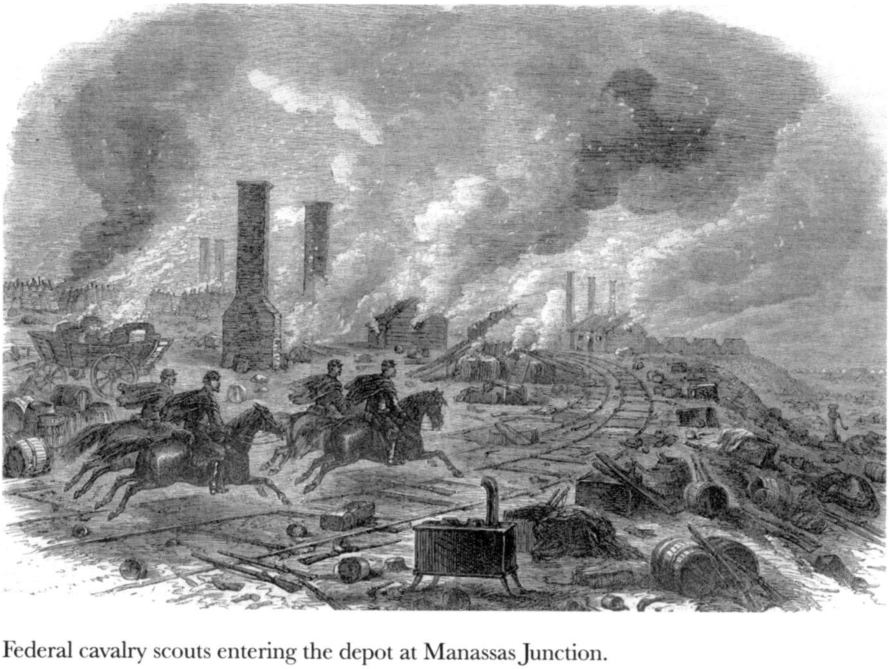

Federal cavalry scouts entering the depot at Manassas Junction.

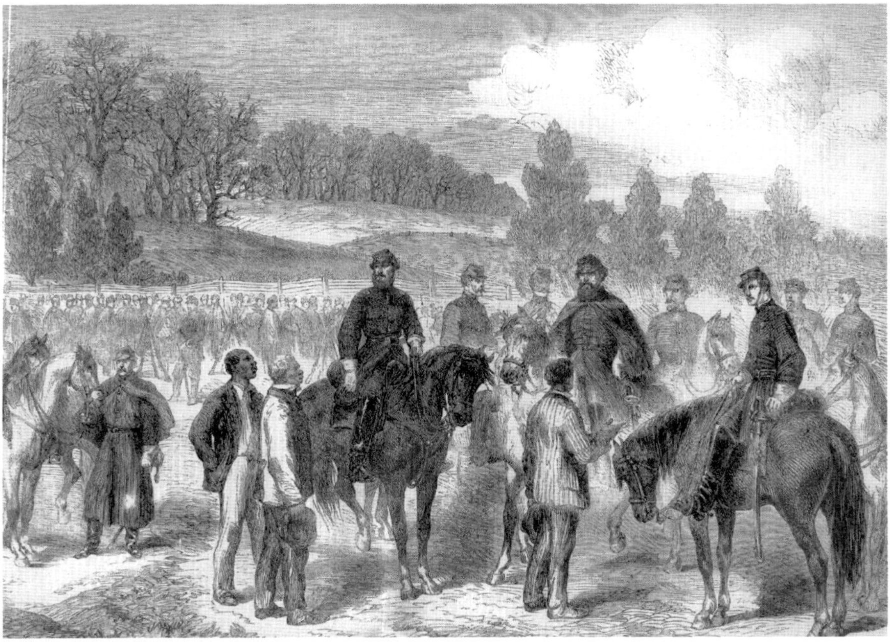

A reconnaissance to Cedar Run made by General Stoneman (center) accompanied by the Comte de Paris (left) and the Duc de Chartres (right).

furor. Vizetelly pondered his options and decided to head to the western theatre. On April 11, he filed a dispatch to send to London, writing:

> *The field will be quite a new one and should I not be followed there with the ban of the Secretary of War upon me, I hope to send you much that will be interesting to your readers. The Western men are proving themselves the heroes of the war, and it appears to me that the opening of the Mississippi will tend greatly to decide the vexed question of Secession that at present divides the North from the South.*
>
> *I leave this evening for the West. There…I shall find field enough for the exercise of my profession where battles, not petty skirmishes of advanced posts, but good, honest, sledge-hammer fights with wholesome bills of mortality, were the order of the day.*

Vizetelly booked train passage to Cairo, Illinois, where the Mississippi and Ohio Rivers join. The Federal base at Cairo was an important springboard for the Union in gaining control of the Mississippi River. In preparation for this campaign on the Mississippi River, Washington had retained the services of James B. Eads, a renowned civil engineer and inventor. Eads had constructed a fleet of seven ironclad gunboats in five months to make ready for this river invasion. These gunboats were designed to ride low in the water. They were constructed of wood but covered with heavy iron plates. They would face an inferior fleet of Confederate ironclads. Without sufficient foundries, the South had to rely on old boilers and railroad iron to plate their ships, leaving them vulnerable to attack with large guns.

General Halleck made plans to take an army down the Mississippi River to Pittsburg Landing and then lead an attack at Corinth, Mississippi. Vizetelly applied to travel with Halleck's army but was refused after General Halleck ordered that civilians would not travel with his army. Vizetelly questioned if "transatlantic journalists are supposed to provide for their own transportation by each man paddling his own canoe."

Fortunately, Vizetelly was able to obtain passage courtesy of the Union navy, traveling with the gunboats heading south. In his dispatch, he wrote of his outlook on the state of affairs with the war:

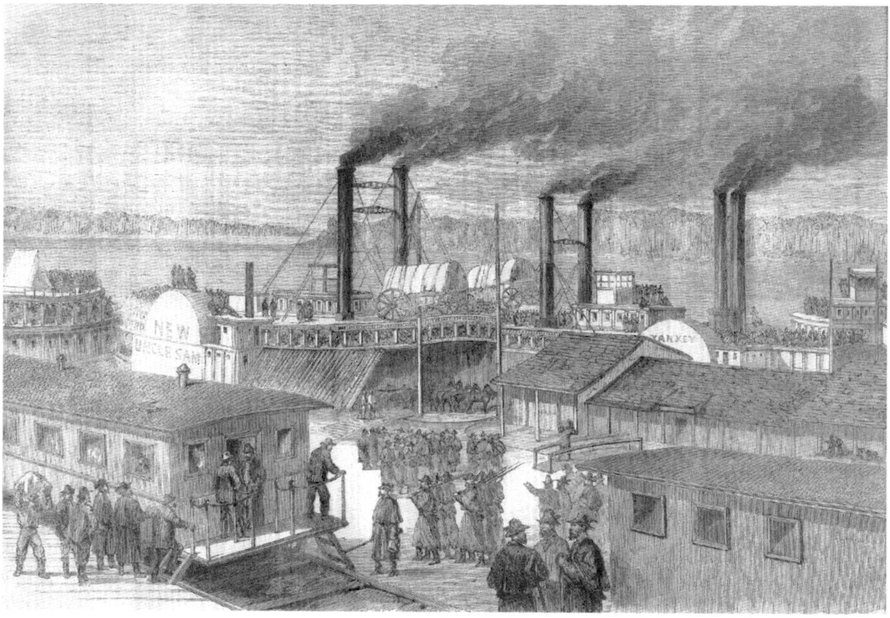

Union general Pope's division at Cairo leaving for New Madrid to reinforce General Halleck.

> *In all conscience, I have had little to thank some of the Federal authorities for lately, and cannot therefore be suspected of any blind partiality; Secession is in a very bad way just now, and a look into the future does not promise much improvement in its condition. The army of the Potomac, that I should have been with, is reaping its laurels by acres in front of Richmond and wiping out the disgrace of Bull Run. Norfolk has fallen; and Burnside with his miniature army, is rapidly closing his grasp on North Carolina. Fort Pulaski has been reduced, and Charleston may at any hour be attacked by Hunter; while the mortar fleet under Porter and Farragut has achieved a most important victory in the capture of New Orleans, the metropolis of the South. The great question in the West is about to be decided in front of Corinth, and, should that place and Richmond fall before the armies of Halleck and McClellan, I see no further hope for the Confederacy.*

Vizetelly went on to discuss the decided advantage of the Union army in provisions, modern arms, foundries to build ironclad gunboats and virtually unlimited supplies of gunpowder. Additionally, many Confederate states had already resorted to conscription while the Federal army was still all-volunteer through mid-1862.

While traveling on the Mississippi River, Vizetelly's boat was attacked by guerillas onshore:

> *This incident happened to the boat on which I have established my headquarters, and the attempt was made on her from the Arkansas shore just above the Chickasaw Bluff. We distinctly saw the rascals, and a strong party was put on shore to capture them, if possible, but they were too well acquainted with the woods, and escaped. We risk at any moment being fired into from the bank; and the unfortunate individual who would attempt to land alone and unarmed on a foraging expedition is almost certain to fall into the hands of these ruffians, for such they should be called from their acts. The chivalrous Southern Confederacy does not appear particular as to the means it employs to attain is ends.*

After six weeks on the river, Vizetelly's next report was filed from the "Federal Flotilla" near Fort Pillow seventy-five miles above Memphis on May 14. He noted that the Mississippi lacked any real shoreline in the conventional sense. While steaming down the Mississippi he saw "nothing but submerged forests for miles and miles back, with here and there a clearing

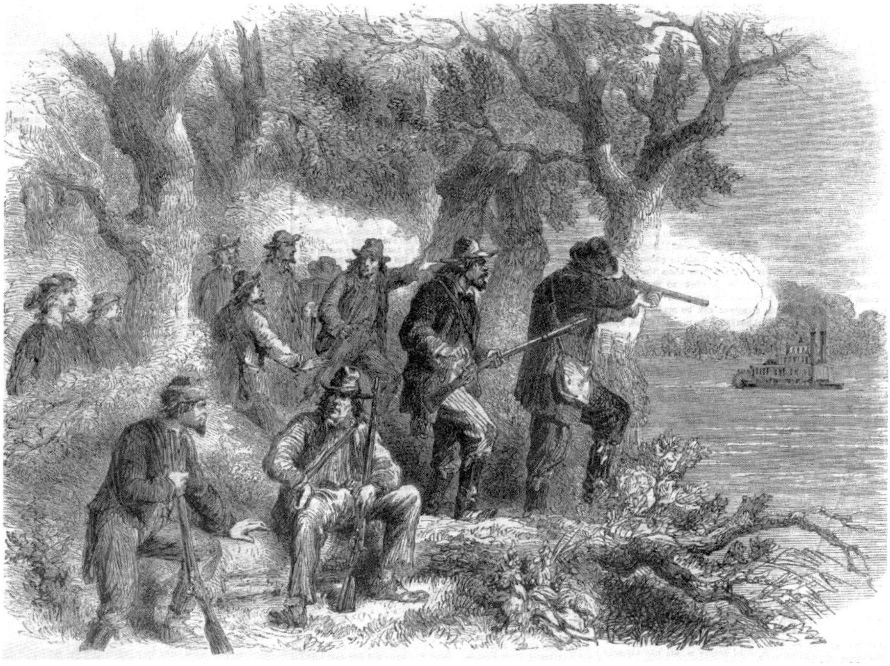

Confederate guerillas shooting at Federal boats on the Mississippi River.

showing the locality of a plantation with the roofs of the planter's house and Negro quarters." The spring thaw in 1862 had caused a much higher than normal water level for the mighty Mississippi, thus running over the banks and into the bordering forests.

Vizetelly arrived just north of Fort Pillow in time to witness the naval attack of the Confederate fortress. Fort Pillow was the main impediment to the Union capture of Memphis. Vizetelly reported:

> *The very morning after my advent, while sitting at breakfast, I was startled by a rapid cannoning all about me. Fort Pillow is on a round bend in the river, some three miles below where we are lying, and beneath its guns the Confederate fleet usually lie for protection…As I rushed to the stern-gallery I saw four of their vessels advancing with a full head of steam on, and not firing a shot, though our boats as they slipped from their moorings to meet them were banging away with their eleven inches gloriously…*
>
> *They* [Confederate gunboats] *were iron-prowed, and handled as rams. In a few minutes they were both onto the* Cincinnati, *striking her*

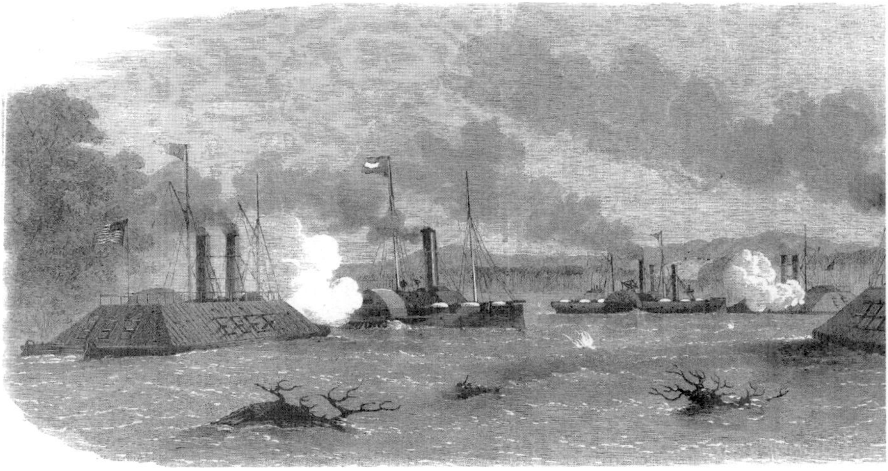

Naval battle between Federal and Confederate gunboats off Fort Pillow on May 10, 1862.

> *with crushing force on her port quarter; before they could get clear she gave them the contents of those of her 10-inch guns that could be trained to bear, both of them drifting down stream, disabled towards Fort Pillow. The* Cincinnati, *whose timbers were completely crushed in, was towed to the shore and grounded to preserve her from sinking; while the* Benton *(flag-boat) advanced to meet the two remaining rams, supported by the* Carondelet. *She gave all her guns in succession to one of them and blew up her boilers, which caused her to drift after her consorts, the other making tracks at full speed. The balance of the Confederate fleet, which had held off, then retired. In addition to the damage to our boats, the Captain of the* Cincinnati *was mortally wounded and the master killed. Three of the Confederate steamers are reported to have sunk after rounding the point.*

Still on the river the next week, Vizetelly wrote of a terrific lightning storm on the Mississippi. He wrote, "It was the most violent storm that I have ever witnessed. The lightning flashed in volumes of flame, succeeded by deafening crashes." During the great storm, it occurred to Vizetelly that he would rather be any place during this storm than on his steamship with an inventory of twenty-five thousand pounds of gunpowder aboard.

As they remained anchored north of Fort Pillow, the Union ships encountered many refugees seeking protection. Vizetelly observed:

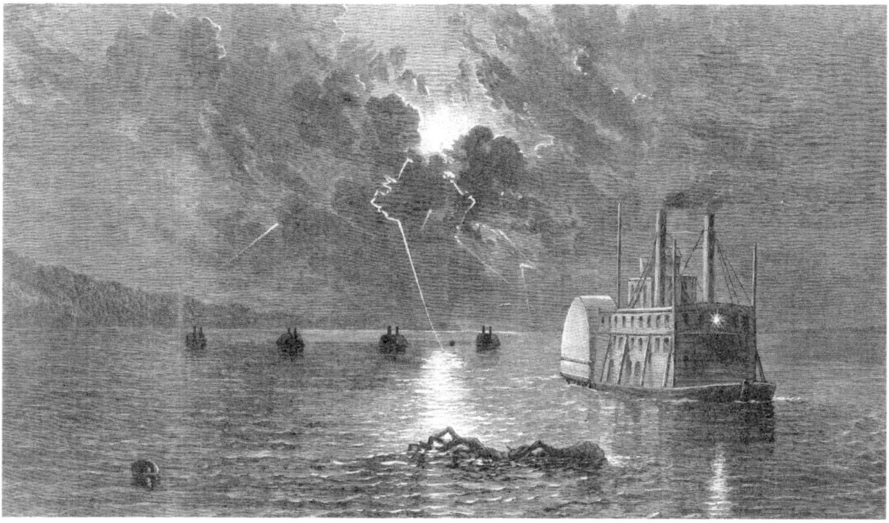

Midnight storm seen from the Federal flotilla anchored off Fort Pillow.

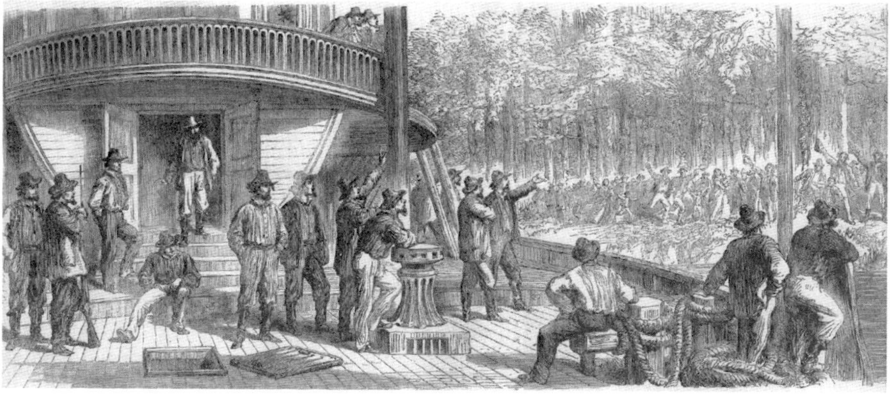

Refugees from Southern cities seeking refuge.

> *Already numbers of refugees from the Confederate strongholds below us have penetrated through the submerged forests in "dug outs," and have requested to be allowed to take the oath of allegiance to the old Government…I cannot conceive they would fly from their homes and seek the protection of Uncle Sam had not their convictions undergone a change, and their confidence in Jeff Davis and his ability to sustain his Government been greatly diminished.*

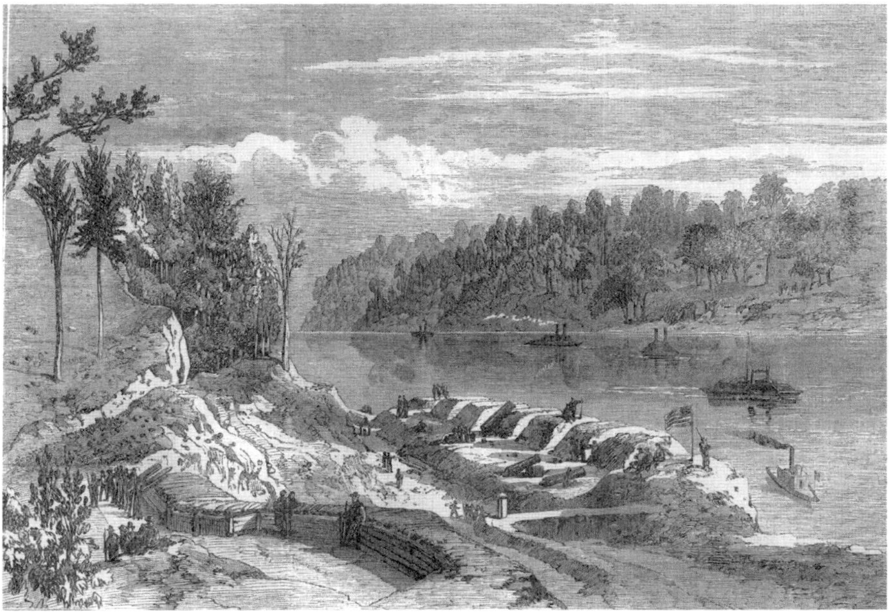

Main battery at Fort Pillow evacuated by the Confederates on June 5, 1862.

The Confederate position at Fort Pillow was able to keep the Federal flotilla from passing their position for almost three weeks. However, the main Confederate army protecting the rear approach to Fort Pillow had to be pulled to reinforce forces at Corinth. This left the fort vulnerable, and on June 4, General Beauregard ordered that the fort be destroyed and the position evacuated as well. Finally, on June 5, the Federal forces with the flotilla occupied Fort Pillow.

This left Memphis as the next target for the Federal fleet. The Federal fleet of nine ironclads moved downriver and anchored three miles above Memphis on the night of June 5. They were hidden from the town by a cluster of islands known by boatmen as "Paddy's Hen and Chickens."

The next morning, the fleet cast off and in thirty minutes rounded the river bend to face a Confederate fleet of eight vessels. The Confederate boats with few guns and those of light caliber were no match for the heavily armored Federal ships. These Confederate boats were designed with reinforced prows to serve as rams. Another feature of these boats was that cotton was used in the bulkhead and interior spaces to protect the ships, earning them the nickname of "cottonclads." In stark contrast to the cottonclads, the Federal ironclads featured between thirteen and sixteen guns apiece.

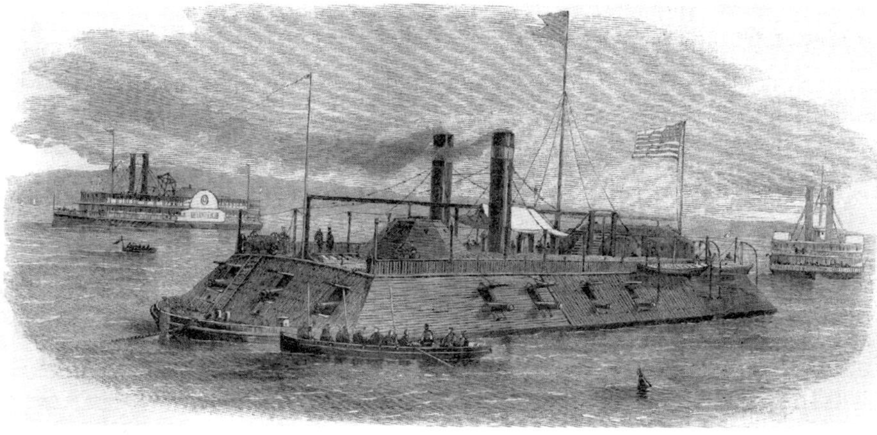

Federal gunboat on the Mississippi River.

Within minutes, all of the gunboats were engaged. In just ninety minutes, three of the eight Confederate gunboats were destroyed and four were captured, and one—the *General Van Dorn*—escaped.

The fall of Memphis cleared the way for the Federal attack on the last Confederate stronghold on the Mississippi River—Vicksburg. Vizetelly disembarked at Memphis with the Federal troops and took a room at the Gayoso House in the city. With the one-hundred-degree temperatures in the day, he was only too happy to be off the ironclad.

From his hotel room, on June 10, he wrote:

> *Memphis, the hotbed of Secession, has fallen. The proud city that would never surrender to the Northern vandal is now garrisoned by Federal soldiers; the blackened, smoking ruins that were to have greeted the advent of the invader was an empty boast; the streets "bathed in blood" but a figurative piece of bombast, for which the editor of* The Appeal *is responsible. Commodore Davis, who commands the national flotilla, need scarcely have wasted words in writing his dispatch. "I came, I saw, I conquered," would have expressed everything. Never was a success so complete and so cheaply purchased by the victors; never an enemy so humiliated. The "stars and bars" have been trailed in the dust; the flag of the Union waves from the principal buildings in the fallen city. Verily, the Memphians have eaten dirt.*

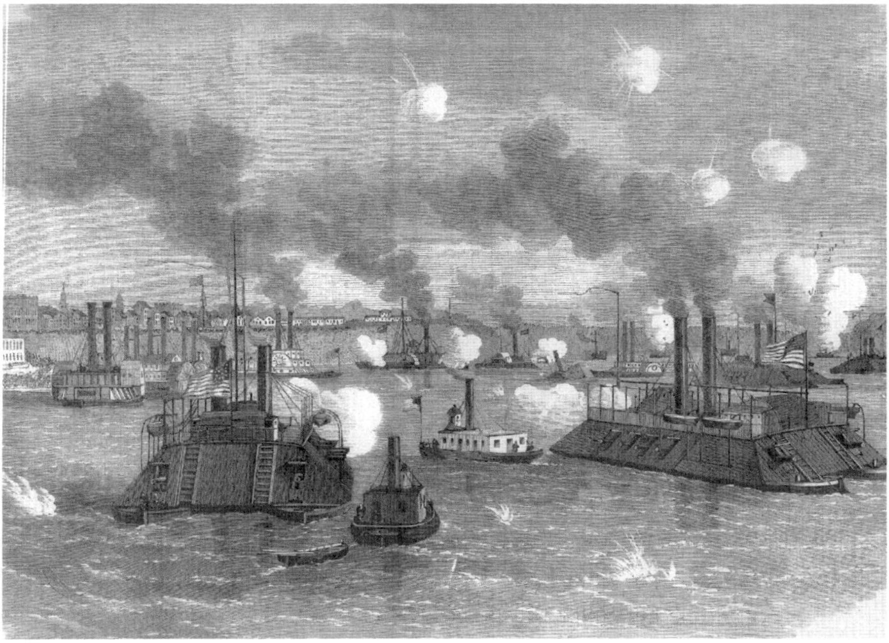

Destruction of the Confederate "cottonclads" off Memphis.

While in Memphis, Vizetelly accompanied a patrol of Federal scouts from the Indiana cavalry to patrol the countryside just outside the city. On one occasion they came upon a plantation where men were burning cotton to keep it from falling into the hands of the Federal army. Cotton was becoming scarce and capturing it was a great war prize. The patrol could not save the cotton but did capture several of the "guerillas" before the group could scatter to the woods.

In Memphis, Vizetelly had his first opportunity to meet and mix with Southerners. He reported:

> *I never saw anything of Southern people until I landed at Memphis...I believed from all I heard that the Secession movement was but skin deep after all, and that the people would willingly return their allegiance to the Government of the United States if the old flag were carried into their midst...I have been astonished at the unanimity displayed by all on the one subject of separation. I am surprised by the bitterness of feeling evinced towards the North by the Memphians. If the entire South is actuated by the same sentiments breathed by the people of south-western Tennessee and*

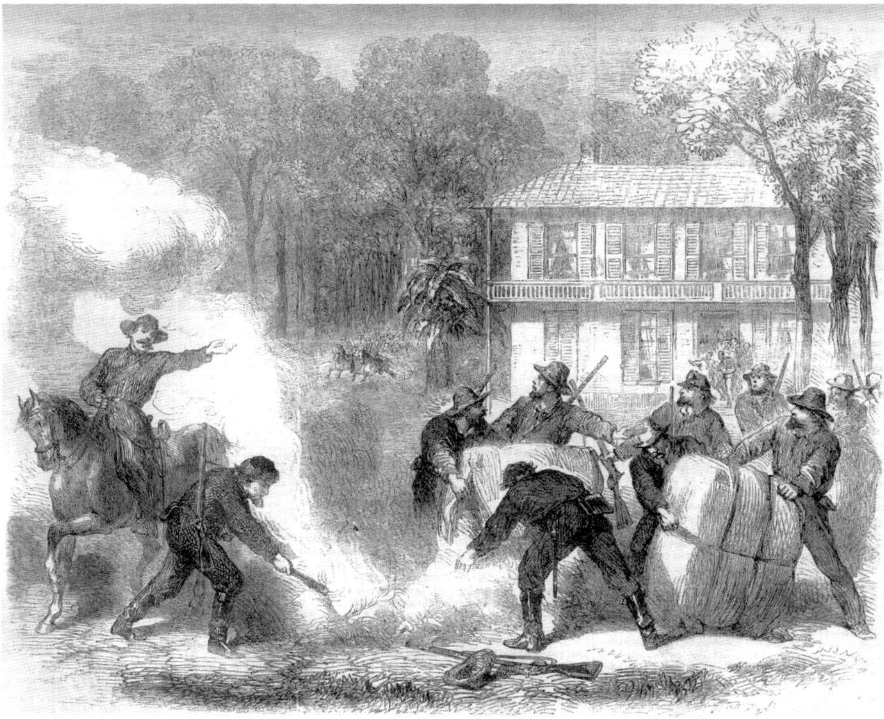

Cotton burners surprised by Federal scouts.

Mississippi, why, then I declare the reconstruction of the Union impossible; and, though the North by superior power and resources may eventually conquer the South, she can never hold her in any other way than which binds Venetia to the Tedeschi [a reference to when Venice was held by the Huns in the fifth century].

Chapter 8

Crossing the Lines

While in the West, Vizetelly got word that Stanton might be relieved of his position as secretary of war. Thinking that he could finally get a permit to travel with the Army of the Potomac, he returned to Washington, only to find out that Stanton was still in office. Nevertheless, he applied for the permit and was once again denied the privilege.

Vizetelly was shocked but intrigued by the deep feeling held by the Southerners he encountered in Memphis. That curiosity and the realization that he may never get access to the Union army in Virginia led Vizetelly to the decision to cross the lines and travel with the Confederate army in Northern Virginia. In July 1862, the British reporter slipped out of the capital city without even notifying his friends and fellow Brits and traveled to Baltimore.

In Baltimore, a source introduced Vizetelly to several Southern sympathizers who agreed to help him cross the lines to join the Confederate army as a correspondent. They secured passage on a river steamboat to travel down the Chesapeake Bay. A stranger led him ashore at Leonard's Town on the north shore of the Potomac River with instructions to find "a Negro buck named Job."

In his memoirs, Henry Vizetelly wrote of the story as told to him by his brother Frank:

> *Under cover of the night Frank Vizetelly and Job attempted to cross the river, but the splashing of their paddle was heard by the watch of a Federal patrol steamer, which fired at them, though fortunately without effect. Job was paralyzed by fright and only came on my brother putting a revolver to his head, when, with his arms flying about like the sails of a windmill, he paddled the "dugout" swiftly back to the Maryland shore, among tall*

rushes, which effectually screened them from observation. For some hours the patrol steamer's search lights continued playing over the river and its banks, but nothing being discovered, the captain cast anchor, evidently purposing to remain in this part of the river until the little craft should emerge from its hiding place. For two nights and one tedious day—tortured by mosquitoes during the former, and roasted by the burning sun during the latter—they remained crouching in their hollow log among the dark reeds, with the patrol boat close by. All this while, too, they were without a particle of food.

When morning broke on the second day my brother noticed that they had drifted down stream under cover of the rushes, and were now some distance from the steamer. To attempt to cross the river was, however, out of the question, though unless they could secure something to eat there would be nothing left for them but to paddle in the open and surrender. Frank Vizetelly questioned Job as to any means there might be of obtaining supplies, but Job only answered with inarticulate moans, till my brother quietly told him he should be obliged to eat him unless he could rouse his torpid brain to suggest some plan for procuring food. Job's wits seem to have been quickened by this threat, for he communicated the welcome information that plenty of remarkably fine oysters were imbedded in the river bank.

No sooner did Frank Vizetelly hear this plan than he sprang out of the cockle-shell craft in search of the bivalves, of which he procured sufficient to calm his own hungry cravings, though not to satisfy the inordinate appetite of the Negro, who, my brother declared, had "a mouth that yawned like a churchyard full of tombstones, but still with an unlimited capacity to bury."

Night again set in, and in the gloaming they rejoiced to see the patrol boat steaming away at full speed towards the river's mouth. As soon as she was well out of sight, they left their hiding place, and in a couple of hours set foot on Virginia soil. My brother then journeyed on to the Rappahannock in the company of a couple of young Marylanders, and having eluded various Federal scouting parties reached Richmond just as the second advance of the Northerners had been repulsed.

In Richmond, Vizetelly took a room at the Spotswood Hotel. His first order of business was to call on F.J. Cridland, the British consul in Richmond. Cridland assisted Vizetelly in presenting his credentials to the Confederate government, which were approved. The reporter had barely settled in before he left to join Robert E. Lee's army on the Rapidan River.

Returning to Richmond on September 20, Vizetelly filed his report to send to the *Illustrated London News*:

> *The North is demoralized by a succession of reverses…The whole Northern people are waiting under the disgrace of continued defeats of the well-equipped armies by, as they themselves term the foe, a half-starved ragged mob of rebels. Defeated on all fronts, the Federals cannot commence a new campaign. Should they try the South will be found prepared, and whatever the result, nobly, I am convinced, will she stem the tide of battle.*

Vizetelly reported that surely soon the readers in England will come to understand "the empty assurances and vain boastings" of the Federal government. His brief experiences with the Southerners had a profound impact on his view of the conflict in America. Union general McClellan's collapse in the Seven Days Battles made quite an impression on the reporter, shaking his belief in the superiority of the Union army. Prior to crossing the lines, Vizetelly referred to the war as the "American Civil War" or the "War of the Rebellion." After spending time with the Confederates and their commanders, the Brit from that point on referred to the war as the "War Between the States."

Vizetelly began writing of his respect for the Confederate army and the people of the South:

> *The more I see of the Southern Army the more I am lost in admiration of its splendid patriotism, at its wonderful endurance, at its utter disregard of hardships which, probably, no modern army has been called upon to bear up against. Wretchedly equipped, the soldiers of the Confederacy advance to meet their foes, the light of battle shining on their countenance, determined to be victorious or die. I have seen them marching over the hot and dirty roads of Virginia, uniformless, shoeless, many with nothing but a thin, well-worn shirt to shelter them from the scorching rays of the sun and yet every man cheered his comrade, and all as they dragged their bleeding feet along made light of their sufferings, and with renewed elasticity strode forward on their way, many to their graves…*
>
> *Surrounded as I am by the Southern people, living in their midst, associating with their soldiers, I emphatically assert that the South can never be subjugated. There is not a mother with two sons, having lost one by a Northern bullet, who would not freely offer up the other on the altar*

> *of her country…Never have I heard a doubtful word expressed as to the ultimate result of the war now waged by the Southerners: every soldier of the Confederacy is impressed with the stamp of individuality, and has confidence in himself which half a million of Northerners cannot shake. And should dire necessity demand that more blood be shed in addition to that which already crimsons the fields of Virginia, Kentucky and Tennessee, there will be five hundred thousand such men ready to form a barricade with their bodies over which the invaders of their soil will have to pass. We have seen the first great Northern army swept away, and the second will scarcely fare better.*

As was his habit, while in Richmond Vizetelly was intimately involved in the social life of his host city. Confederate officers described the reporter as "a large man with a great red beard and a hearty, captivating personality." Vizetelly often hosted great dinners during which he told stories, sang songs and danced. His frequent guests included the Confederate hierarchy and many of the visiting British officials, including Colonel Henry Charles Fletcher, Colonel George Gordon, Captain Frank W. Dawson, Lord Charles Cavendish and Francis C. Lawley with the London *Telegraph.*

Vizetelly was with Lee's army in August 1862 for the Battle of Second Manassas. The battle was fought on the same ground as First Manassas but, this time, with much larger armies. After the Seven Days Battles, Lincoln replaced McClellan with Major General John Pope as the commander of the Union Army of Virginia. Pope, with sixty-two thousand troops, was facing Lee's army of fifty thousand men in familiar territory near Gordonsville, Centreville and Manassas.

Stonewall Jackson flanked the Union army and captured its supply depot at Manassas Junction. After several maneuvers, Pope mistakenly thought that he had trapped Jackson and on August 29 launched a series of attacks on Jackson's position. By noon of that same day, Confederate general Longstreet arrived and set his army on Jackson's right flank.

The next day, Pope renewed his attack but was unaware of Longstreet's arrival. Confederate artillery stalled a Union assault led by Major General Fitz John Porter's corps, and Longstreet's twenty-five thousand men counterattacked and crushed the Union left flank. Defeated, Pope had to withdraw his army to Centreville.

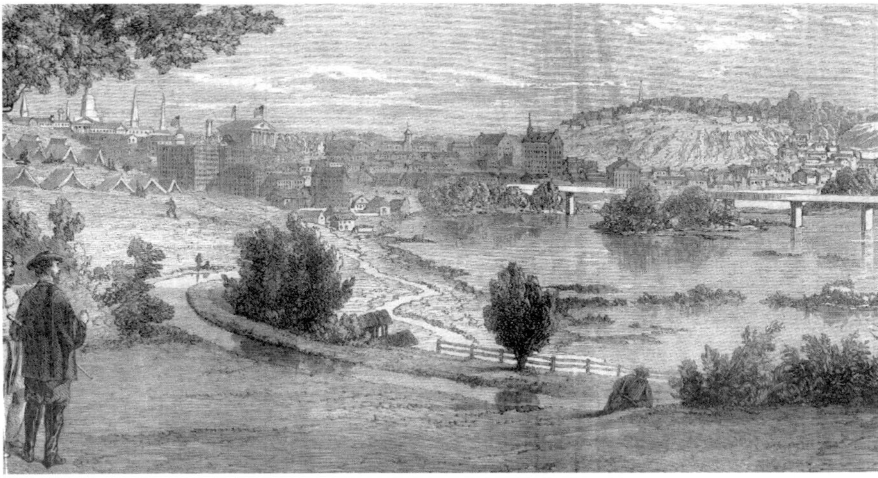

View of Richmond from the west. Vizetelly sketched his own image on the far left of the illustration.

Vizetelly was there to sketch the battle and report:

> *The Yankee army, towards the close of the day, sought refuge in a gully near the Alexandria and Orange Railroad. For some hours they fought against the Confederates, who used stones and rocks, their ammunition exhausted. The Confederates kept the Federals off, and eventually remained masters of the field. The engraving shows the division of General Longstreet charging with the bayonet against the masses assembled to stay the triumphant progress of the Southern arms.*

By mid-October 1862, Vizetelly had established a friendship with the flamboyant Confederate cavalry commander General J.E.B. Stuart. The reporter spent much of his time in camp with Stuart and his senior command. He sketched Stuart leading a scouting party and skirmishing with Pope's army near Culpepper Courthouse. Stuart had become famous in England earlier as Vizetelly had written of his raids on McClellan's army while threatening Richmond. Vizetelly's engraving featured Stuart at the front of the column.

Stuart and his men loved having the always entertaining reporter in their camp. Even the black cooks and porters in the Confederate camp, who called Vizetelly "Major Telly," thoroughly enjoyed his tales and songs. Major Heros von Borcke of the Prussian army, who was riding with Stuart, wrote of Vizetelly:

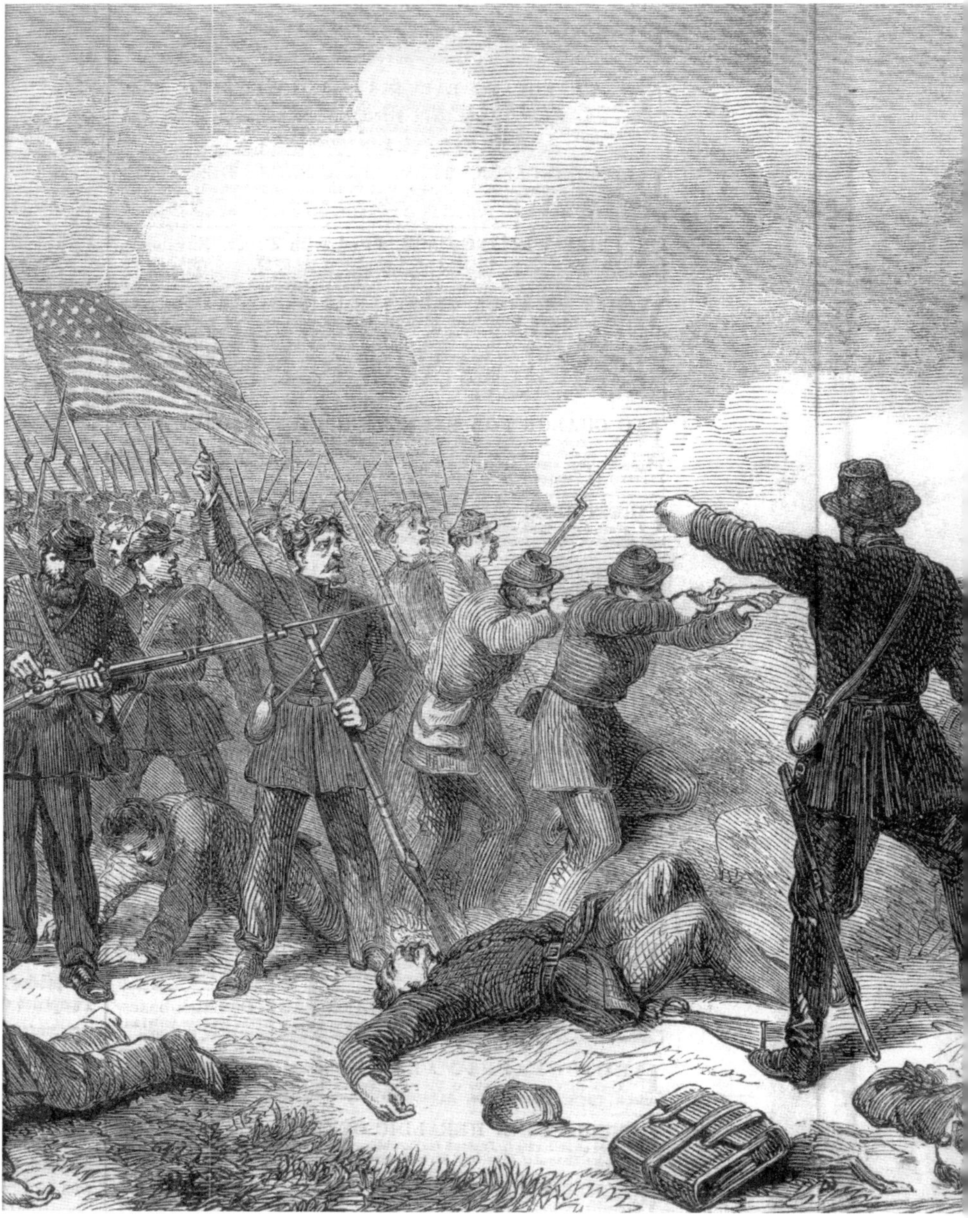

The last stand made by the Federal troops at Manassas.

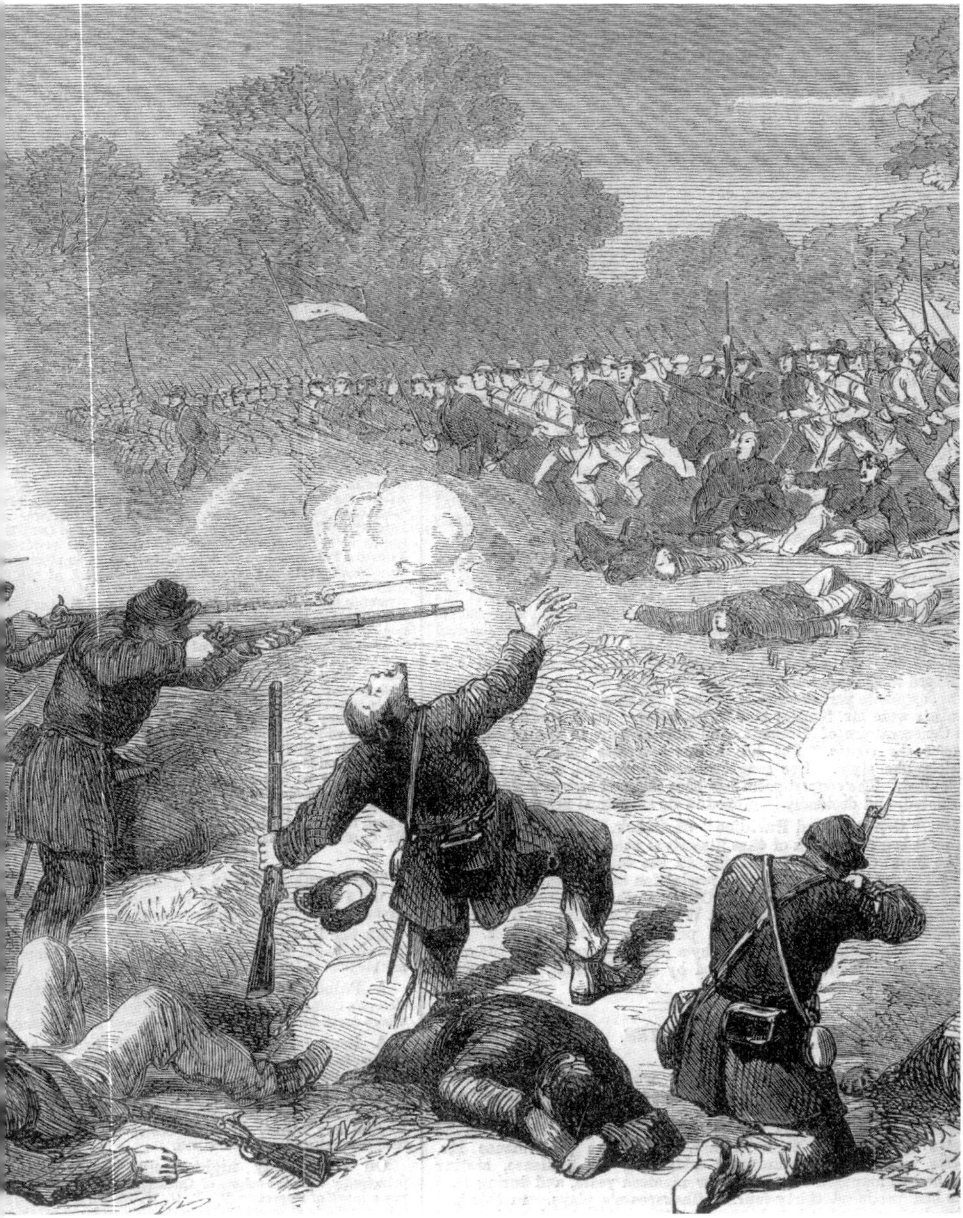

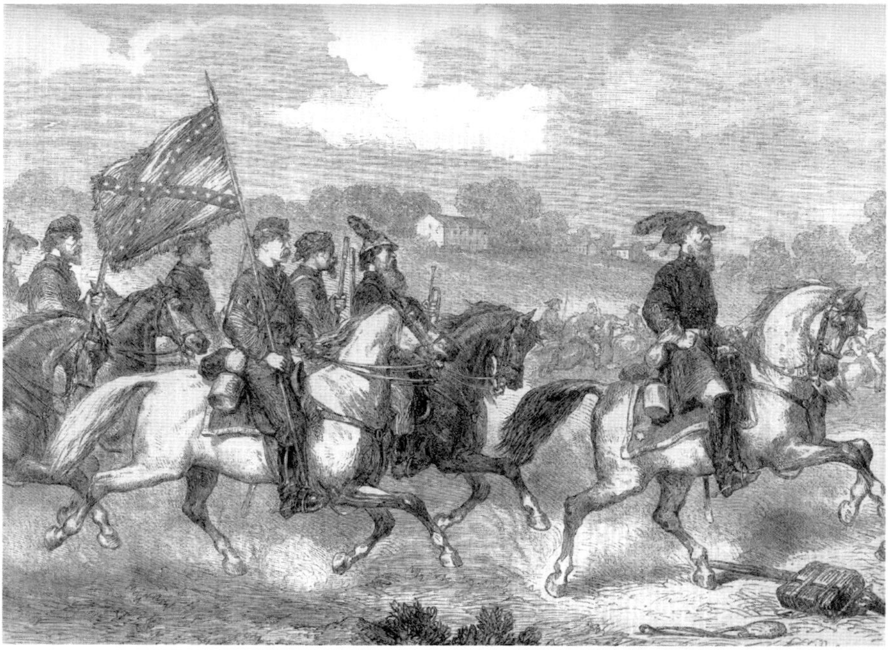

Confederate scouting party led by General J.E.B. Stuart.

Our new guest was an old campaigner, who accommodated himself very readily to the hardships of camp life, and was soon established in his own tent, which I caused to be erected for him in the immediate neighborhood of Blackford and myself. He was not long in becoming a general favorite at headquarters. Regularly after dinner, our whole family of officers, from commander down to the youngest lieutenant, used to assemble in his tent, squeezing ourselves into narrow quarters to hear his entertaining narratives, which may possibly have received a little embellishment in the telling, but which embraced a very wide circle of human experience, and had a certain ease and brilliancy beyond most recitals. The "ingenuous youth" of our little circle drank in delightedly the intoxication of Mabile and Shateau des Fleurs, or followed the story-teller with eager interest as he passed from the gardens and the boudoirs of Paris to the stirring incidents and picturesque scenery of the Italian campaign, which he had witnessed as guest of Garibaldi. Vizetelly was greatly pleased with our musical entertainments; and when, from the gathering darkness, we could only distinguish the place where he was reclining by the glow of his pipe, and thus lost all the play

> *of the features of his rehearsal, we proceeded to our great central camp-fire, there to renew the Negro dances to the music of the banjo—scenes which Vizetelly's clever pencil has placed before the European public in the pages of the* Illustrated London News.
>
> *Less successful was our friend in his efforts to improve the cuisine of our Negro camp cook, and we often had the laugh upon him—especially when one day he produced in triumph a roast pig, with the conventional apple in his mouth, which we found to be raw on one side and burnt to a cinder on the other. The work of art had been prepared under his personal management, and was served as* cochon a' l'Italienne, *but it proved by no means as happy an accident as the original roast pig, done* a' la Chinoise.

Lieutenant Colonel William Blackford, Stuart's adjutant, also wrote of Vizetelly's visits:

> [On October 16, 1862,] *within a mile of the Bower they* [General Stuart and staff] *withdrew a mile and went into camp. Satisfied that this was all for that day General Stuart made the proper dispositions of his force and we returned to the hospitable Bower, its cordial welcome*

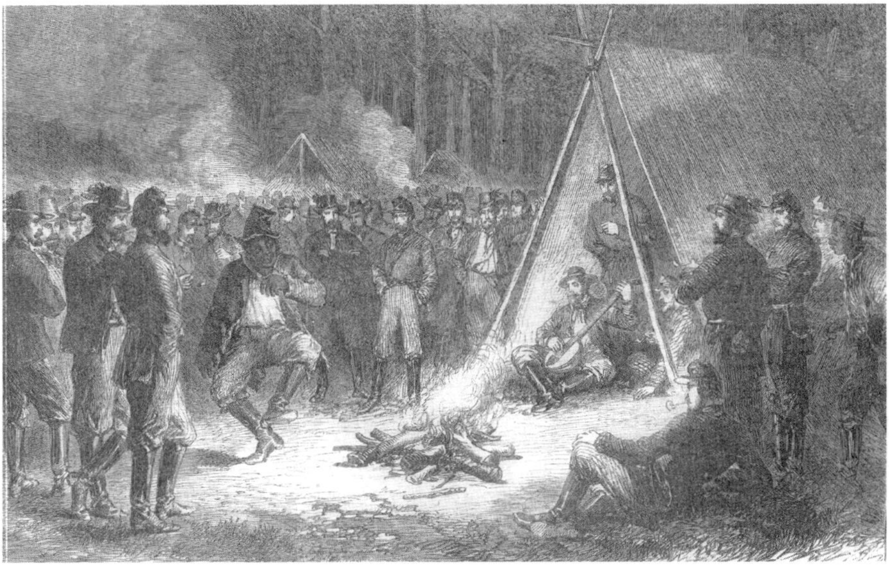

Night amusements in the Confederate camp.

> *and its cheerful fireside. Here we found two Englishmen come on a visit to headquarters. The Honorable Francis Lawley H.C. and Mr. Frank Vizetelly, correspondent of the* Illustrated London News. *Mr. Lawley was the correspondent of the London* Times. *These gentlemen were often after this our guests, and we all became fond of them…*
>
> *Vizetelly was the most interesting narrator I have ever listened to around a campfire. He had been in all parts of the world, and in several campaigns as a correspondent, and what he did not see and enjoy of social life of every grade was not worth seeing. There was not a disreputable or reputable place of prominence in the civilized world that he did not know about, and his accounts of his gallantries in Paris and other parts of the world were as interesting as a novel.*
>
> *We had a shrewd suspicion that he drew a little on his imagination for his facts, but what difference did that make to us. Late into the night we all sat around the embers of our fire out under the grand oaks listening to the fascinating tales he told, his expressive countenance and gestures giving full effect to his words by their play. Mr. Lawley was an exceedingly intelligent and refined Englishman and in another style we enjoyed his instructive conversation very much, but Vizetelly was fascinating.*

In November 1862, Vizetelly left Stuart to go to the Blue Ridge Mountains. When he returned, the entire camp broke out in the tune of "Dixie" but using new words that Vizetelly composed, all to the great delight of the Englishman.

Chapter 9

The Battle of Fredericksburg

In November 1862, Union general Ambrose Burnside was named commander of the Army of the Potomac, replacing General McClellan. Lincoln and General in Chief Major General Henry W. Halleck instructed Burnside to initiate a late fall offensive. Burnside planned to stage a large force on Union troops feigning a move to Gordonsville but quickly shift to march on the Rappahannock River and cross to Fredericksburg.

Burnside organized the Army of the Potomac into three large divisions totaling 114,000 troops, with a corps of 6,000 men to be held in reserve, part at Fairfax Court House and part at Harpers Ferry. They would face Lee's Army of Northern Virginia totaling 85,000 men.

Vizetelly was with General Longstreet's corps as he moved his force across the Blue Ridge from the Shenandoah Valley to the Rappahannock. Jackson would command the Second Corps for Lee, added to the Reserve Artillery under Brigadier General William Pendleton and the cavalry under Major General Stuart. Vizetelly wrote of Longstreet's passage:

> *Of the entire Confederate army encamped near Winchester, Jackson's corps alone remains, and that, I presume, will soon follow the main body into Loudoun County, where Burnside menaces with an immense army the line of the Rappahannock in this, the third, advance of the Federals on Richmond. The subject of the Engraving is one of the picturesque passes in the Blue Ridge, with General Longstreet's corps-d'armee passing through on its way to Culpepper to hold in check the Northern forces. The scenery of these Virginian Mountains reminds me forcibly of the Apennines, and recalls many scenes which I have witnessed with Garibaldi's forces in Southern Italy.*

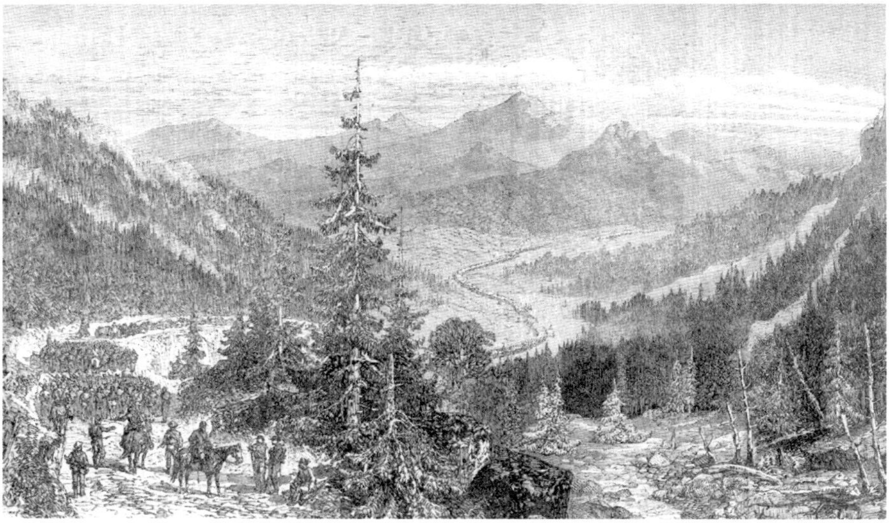

General Longstreet's corps crossing the Blue Ridge from the Shenandoah to the Rappahannock.

The Army of the Potomac began moving on November 15 with the first troops arriving at Falmouth, less than two miles from Fredericksburg, two days later. Immediately, Burnside's plan was in jeopardy as the pontoon bridges needed to cross the Rappahannock did not arrive with the advance regiments of his army. Major General Edwin "Bull" Sumner, commander of one of the three divisions, suggested that his men ford the river and occupy the town. Burnside was concerned that in the event of strong rains Sumner could become stranded in the town before the other divisions could cross. He ordered Sumner to remain in Falmouth.

Vizetelly rode to Fredericksburg with Major von Borcke to conduct a reconnaissance in order to, as Vizetelly put it, "take a good look at the town and at our Yankee friends on the opposite side of the river."

Vizetelly offered a detailed report of the small Virginia town for the European readers:

> *The little town of Fredericksburg had previously suffered rough usage, having been in the hands of Confederates and Federals two or three times. It is the chief town of Spotsylvania county, Virginia, and is situated on the right bank of the Rappahannock River, at the head of tide-water. It is between 50 and 60 miles from Richmond by railroad, and 65 miles by the turnpike, in a northerly direction. The town is pleasantly situated in*

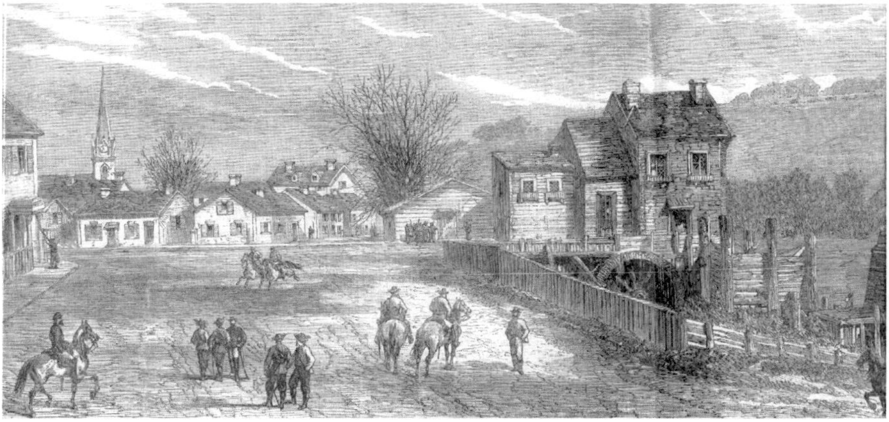

The position of Federal and Confederate pickets at Fredericksburg on December 4, 1862.

> *a fertile valley, and has advantages for commerce and manufactures. The railroad from Washington, via Acquia Creek, passes through it, and as the through-trains generally stop at Fredericksburg Station for about an hour on each trip, a not inconsiderable chance trade was caused thereby in the immediate locality of the depot. A good canal has been constructed from the town to a point on the Rappahannock River about 40 miles above, by which large quantities of wheat, flour, and tobacco were formerly received for exportation. The river affords extensive water power, which, however, has not been much used. The hills in the neighborhood, varying from 40 to 100 feet high, abound in fine granite and freestone…*
>
> *The correspondent of the New York Times reports: "It is 'living' Fredericksburg 'no more.' A city, soulless, rent by the wrack of war."*

Burnside wanted to cross the river ten miles downstream at Skinker's Neck, but Confederate general Early had already arrived there. Burnside then decided to cross directly at Fredericksburg. On December 9, Burnside reported to Halleck, "I think now the enemy will be more surprised by a crossing immediately in our front than at any other part of the river."

Lee deployed Longstreet on the left flank, positioned on a ridge named Marye's Heights. The rest of the Confederate army was deployed south of the city under Jackson. Vizetelly was positioned at Fredericksburg the morning on December 11, writing, "It is whispered at head-quarters today that an attempt will be made by the enemy to cross the river at three different points during the night. I am lying out in the pine-woods at the advance,

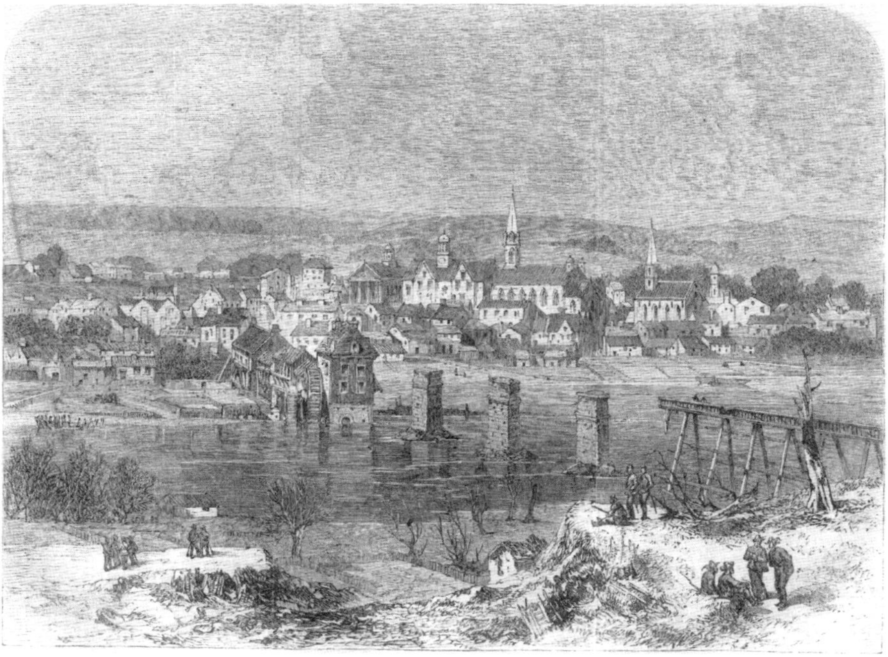

Scene of the Battle of Fredericksburg after the Federal bombardment of the town.

ready to wield my pencil when the struggle begins. Every shot we hear as we lie with our feet to the fire during the long cold nights starts us on our legs."

The morning of December 11, Union engineers began assembling six pontoon bridges at the Rappahannock but came under intense fire from Confederate sharpshooters. Burnside was convinced to send his troops across in boats during the night to raid the sharpshooters. Union artillery pummeled the town with more than five thousand shells. The bridges were then completed, and the Federals stormed into town, looting and destroying the property they encountered.

The battle started at 8:30 a.m. on the morning of December 13 when Union general Franklin attacked Jackson's defenses. The assaults west of Fredericksburg began at 11:00 a.m. with French's division. A critical tactical error resulted when the Union troops were forced to move in two columns over two small bridges, effectively leaving them at the mercy of the Confederate guns. With French repulsed, Burnside sent in Hancock and Howard's divisions under Sumner, but they faced Longstreet's strong position at Mayre's Heights.

Vizetelly watched the fight from the Confederate field headquarters, writing, "From the point where I stood, with Generals Lee and Longstreet, I could see the grape, shell, and canister from the guns…mow great avenues in the masses of Federal troops rushing to the assault, while the infantry… decimated the nearest columns." While watching the intensity of the battle at its height, Lee was quoted as remarking, "It is well that war is so terrible, or we should grow too fond of it."

Many of the Union troops were trapped on the fields leading to Marye's Heights but could not advance or retreat due to the intense fire from the Confederates. Both armies remained in place on the next day. Burnside contemplated one more attack on Marye's Heights, but his officers urged him to withdraw, which he ultimately did.

Through the course of the multiple-day battle, Burnside launched sixteen individual charges, one at a time, that all failed. These frontal assaults on Marye's Heights and Prospect Hill resulted in devastating casualties. Union general Meade did penetrate Jackson's line briefly on the Union left flank but was quickly repulsed by a counterattack.

Both armies lost key officers in the battle. Union general C. Feger Jackson commanding a brigade under General Meade was killed along with his aide during one Confederate volley. Union general George Bayard was a cavalry officer that led the attack at Fredericksburg, at which he was injured by a shell fragment and died the following day, just days short of his intended wedding. Confederate general Thomas R.R. Cobb, commander of Cobb's Legion, was mortally wounded by a Federal shell fragment at Marye's Heights. General Maxey Gregg, commander of a brigade under Jackson, was shot in the spine while mounting his horse during an attack and died two days later.

Union casualties totaled 13,353 compared to only 4,576 for the Confederates. When Vizetelly walked the fields in front of Marye's Heights where the Union assault stalled, he wrote:

> *I counted 660 dead lying on a small plot of ground, scarcely four acres in extent, at the foot of the hill…; and altogether 1493 were buried between the hill and that part of town. Eight hundred were buried on that part of the field occupied by Franklin. These were all Federals…The Federals, beside this, buried many within their own lines on the night of the battle.*

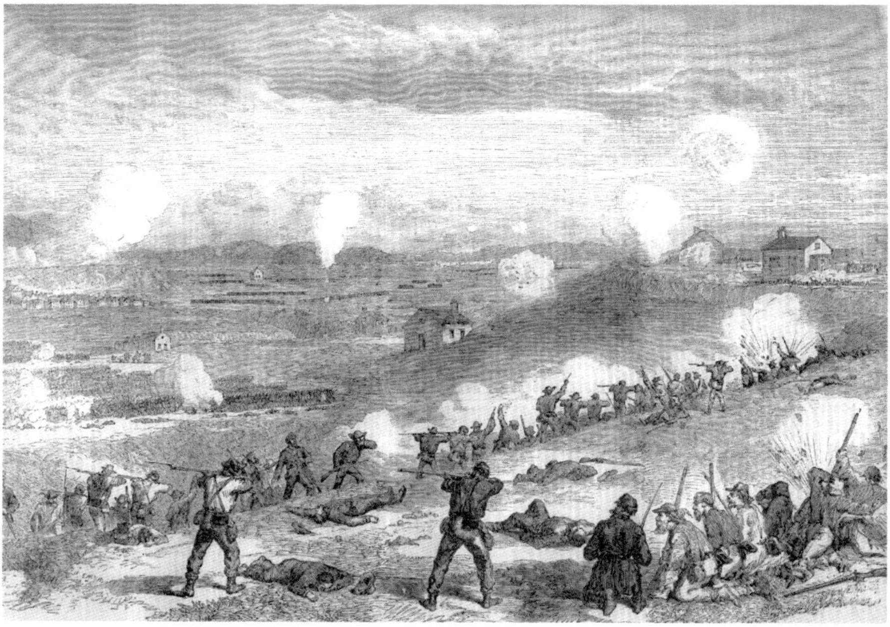

The Battle of Fredericksburg—assault of the Federal army on Mabry's Hill.

After the battle, Vizetelly described Virginia as "a classic ground, crimsoned with deeds that will make history for the future."

Vizetelly noted that the Confederates also had their share of fun, as he witnessed a massive snowball fight between divisions after Fredericksburg. He observed men dancing around the campfires at night, attempting to sing the London songs he endeavored to teach them. Still, the harsh reality of war was never distant as all thought of friends lost in battle "in the awful drama that has spread desolation over many a once smiling acre of Virginia soil...In many a distant clump of pine wood slept their last sleep those whom I had known in life. *Requiescat in pace.*"

Traveling with the Confederate army posed a logistical problem for Vizetelly. When he was traveling with Union troops, he simply dispatched his reports and sketches to Washington, knowing that they would find safe passage to his London editors. Now that he was behind the Confederate lines, he had to send his work aboard blockade runners, hoping that they would get through to London. Valuing his work, *Harper's Weekly* offered Union naval officers a bounty if they captured any Vizetelly sketches aboard detained ships.

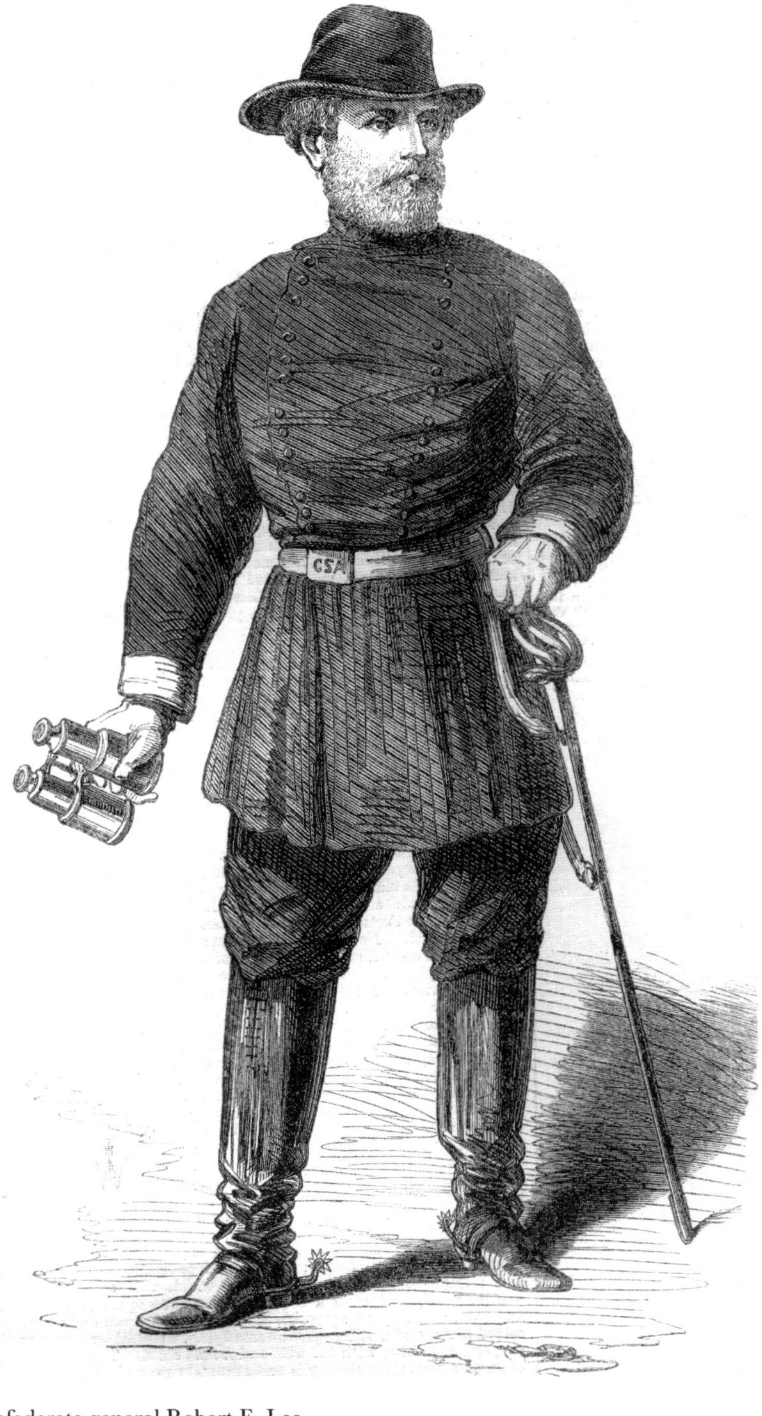

Confederate general Robert E. Lee.

Vizetelly did get a letter through to London asking why his sketches of Jackson's headquarters, Lee's headquarters, an encampment of Confederates on the Shenandoah, views of Winchester and others had not appeared. He learned that the paper never received them. The editor of the *Illustrated London News* finally wrote to assure his readers anxious for news from America that the failure to publish engravings was from "no lack or spirit or industry on the part of our special artist."

Vizetelly did manage to get sketches and letters about Robert E. Lee, Stonewall Jackson and J.E.B. Stuart through the blockade. In his report, Vizetelly noted that Lee "wears his years well and strikes you as the incarnation of health and endurance." It is no small irony that as Vizetelly wrote this Lee was actually suffering from heart disease and high blood pressure. He continued, "On the rare occasion when he smiles, and on still rarer occasions when he laughs heartily…the confidence and sympathy which he inspires are irresistible."

Lee made a marked impression on Vizetelly:

> *It is impossible to converse for ten minutes without perceiving how deeply he has meditated upon all the possible eventualities of the campaign in Virginia, and how sound and well-considered are the positions which he advances. It is obvious that the most entire and trusting confidence is placed in General Lee by his subordinate officers, whose respect and affection he seems thoroughly to have won.*

Vizetelly talked Lee into wearing his full battle uniform, including his sword, while sketching him, the only such engraving of Lee during the war. The reporter observed that typically "he is exceedingly plain in his dress, and you look at his costume in vain for the insignia of rank…He cares but little for appearances."

After the engraving appeared in the *Illustrated London News*, Lee sent a copy to his wife, writing, "A likeness of your husband has come from beyond the big water. I hope his beard will please you, for the artist seems to have laid himself out on that. We are poor judges of ourselves and I cannot therefore pronounce as to his success."

Once the London issue with Lee's likeness reached the United States, *Harper's Weekly* republished the sketch in their newspaper. The same issue of the *Illustrated London News* also published Vizetelly's sketch and letter about Stonewall Jackson:

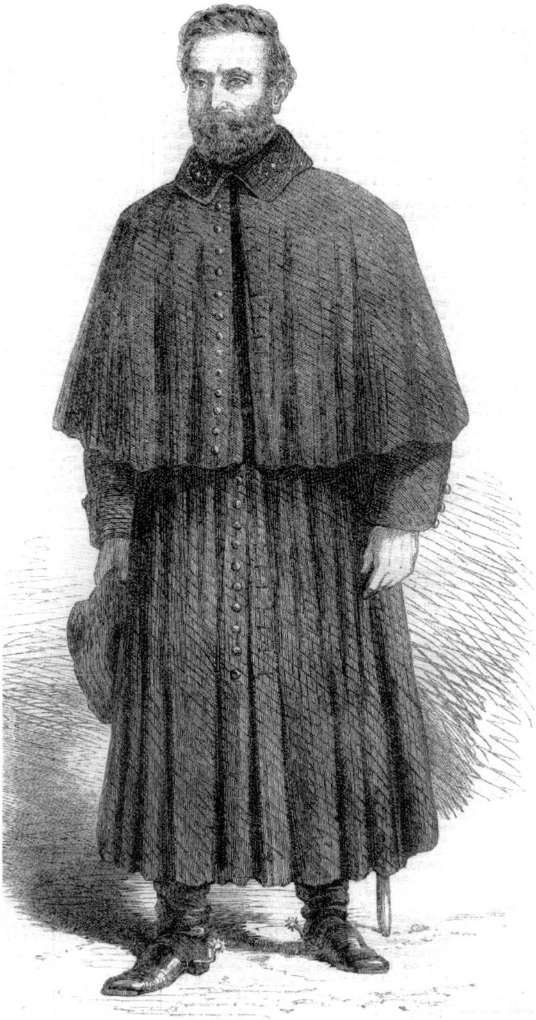

Confederate general Thomas "Stonewall" Jackson.

At a distance of seven miles from General Lee's head-quarters...were the head-quarters of "Stonewall" Jackson. I had been taught to expect a morose, reserved, distant reception; I found the most genial, courteous, and forthcoming of companions. A bright piercing blue eye, a slightly aquiline nose, a thin, tall sinewy frame "made all over of pinwire," a great disregard of dress and appearance—these are the characteristics of General Jackson's exterior. There is also about him a very direct and honest look. The disappointing circumstance is that his voice, which is rapid in its utterance, is weak and unimpressive. Passionately attached to the Valley of

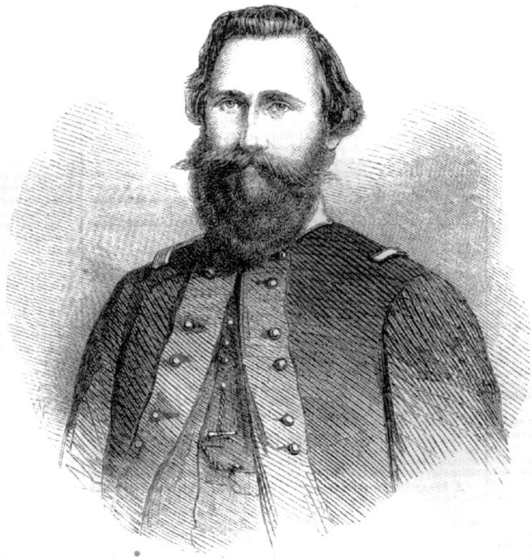

Confederate general J.E.B. Stuart.

Virginia, which has for so long been the principal scene of his achievements, idolized by the inhabitants of Winchester and of the valley, General Jackson has acquired such a fame in that entire neighborhood that it is sad to think what would happen if the one life round which such prestige clings should yield to a stray bullet or to the chance of disease. Sinewy and wiry as the General seems, it is impossible not to fancy that he is wearing himself terribly by his restless, sleepless activity, by his midnight marches, and by the asceticism of his life. The respect and consciousness of his presence, and what that presence means, exhibited by his staff, impressed me very strongly, and seemed to exceed the respect exhibited towards General Lee.

While Lee may have liked his engraving, he did not care for the one of Jackson, noting that it "failed to give his firm candid and frank expression, so charming to see and so attractive to the beholder."

The following week, the newspaper published Vizetelly's sketch of General J.E.B. Stuart, referring to the cavalry officer as "the Murat of the Confederates; their Prince Rupert, with more than that Prince's success."

Vizetelly wrote of Stuart:

The twenty-nine years of General Stuart, added to that that indefatigable energy which teaches him, after he has ridden fifty miles during the day, to regard it as his highest happiness to ride a dozen more miles at night "to tread but one measure" in a Virginian country-house, do not incline the scale, especially if the balance be adjusted by fair hands, in favour of the younger General. There have been many English officers, particularly in the East Indian service, whose endurance in the saddle has been regarded as unequalled; but I doubt whether any Englishman ever exhibited such superiority to bodily fatigue as is almost nightly evinced by the gay cavalier who knows every hospitable roof within a dozen miles of his head-quarters, and, accompanied by his banjo player, visits them by night after night, returning usually to his hard-earned rest long after the midnight hour has flown.

With the earliest dawn of morning the first voice calling gaily for breakfast is that of the midnight merrymaker, who rises the picture of health, good humor, and strength. It may be noticed en passant that to the circumstance that he has never touched tobacco in any form, nor wine or other liquor, to which General Stuart attributes much of his health and vigor. Certainly so jovial a company as is assembled at General Stuart's headquarters it has never been my fortune to see paralleled in either the Federal or Confederate camps.

Chapter 10

In the Heart of Secessia

In January 1863, Vizetelly made his way to Charleston, South Carolina, anxious to visit the city where the secession movement began. He took a room at the Charleston Hotel on Meeting Street and immediately set up an appointment to meet with General P.G.T. Beauregard to present his credentials.

In September 1862, Beauregard was named as commander for the Department of South Carolina, Georgia and Florida and returned to Charleston to further enhance the defenses of the city. When Vizetelly arrived, Beauregard and General Roswell Ripley, commander of the First Military District, South Carolina, had stationed ten thousand troops in Charleston to anticipate the inevitable return of the Union army to the city.

Vizetelly immediately began sketching the city and the Confederate defenses. On January 20, Vizetelly accompanied Ripley on an inspection of the troops at Fort Sumter:

> *The war which has raged so long and fiercely throughout the States began, as our readers are aware, by the bombardment, just two years ago, of Fort Sumter in Charleston Harbor, South Carolina—a bloodless engagement, little indicative of the seas of blood which were and, it is to be feared, still are to be shed. Public attention has been again directed in a special manner to Charleston on account of the recent dashing attack of Confederate gun-boats on the Federal blockading squadron off the harbour, and by reason also of the news just received that a formidable land and naval expedition was about to attack Charleston forthwith.*

Vizetelly would not disclose details about the defenses of Charleston, knowing that the Federal command, like everyone else interested in the

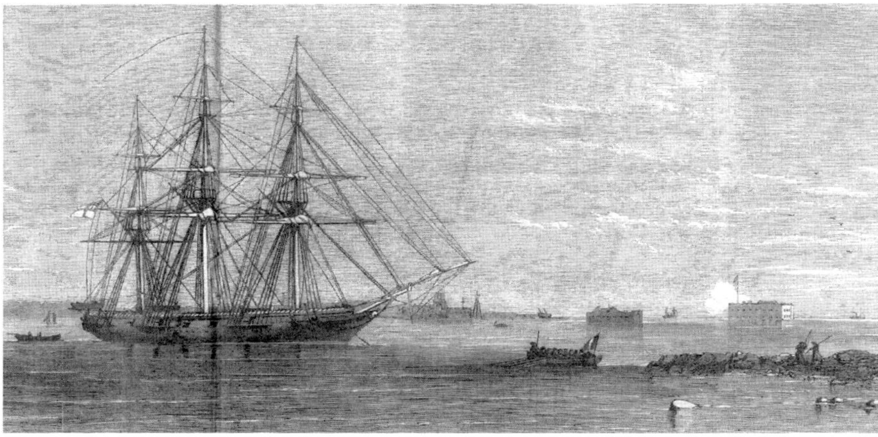

Charleston Harbor. Fort Sumter is located on the right.

war, followed the accounts published in his newspaper. Instead, the paper published the details of the Charleston fortifications that were previously published in various newspapers in 1861. The paper's editor wrote, "Our artist, 'incommunicable elf,' preserves a profound silence, on the plea—a valid one, doubtless—that he was bound in honor not to divulge secrets entrusted to him in confidence."

Again, Vizetelly experienced great difficulty getting his sketches and reports through the blockade. The editor of the *Illustrated London News* noted that the North "has succeeded, with its great resources, in isolating the South from all but the sympathy of Europe...The gentleman who has for some time past acted as our Special Artist and Correspondent in the Southern States of America finds the greatest difficulty in sending us the results of his labours."

Two sketches made by Vizetelly from Fort Johnson on James Island did get through the blockade:

> *Now, all these batteries combined, and many others that have been added have improved and strengthened to such an extent that it seems impossible that anything can enter the harbor. I have not drawn all the defenses, because I am bound in honour not to divulge them. They will, however, be discovered by the Federal ships whenever they attempt to force a passage.*

Again, once *Harper's Weekly* received copies of the latest issue of the *Illustrated London News*, it copied the illustrations of the Charleston defenses.

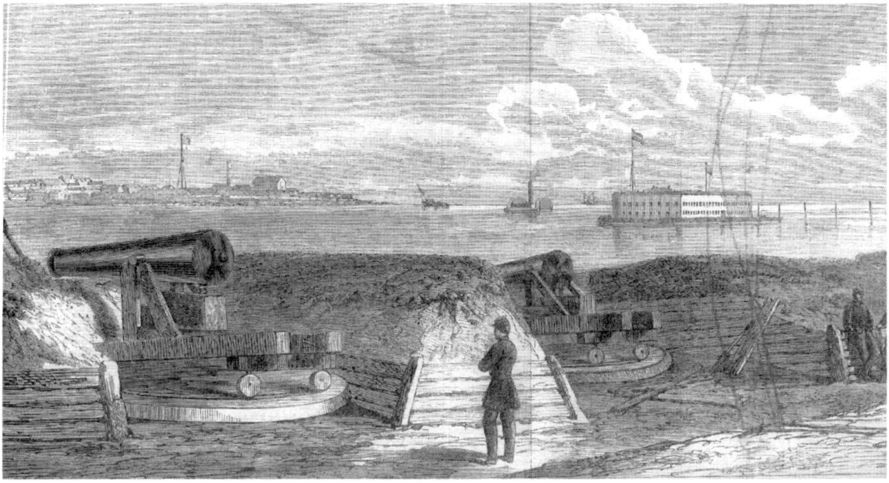

View of Fort Sumter (right) and Sullivan's Island (left) from Fort Johnson on James Island.

The publication was even so bold as to credit Vizetelly, but not the *News*, for the work it now plagiarized. The New York paper wrote:

> *We publish…two illustrations of Charleston, from sketches made for a London paper by Mr. Vizetelly, who is now in Secessia. Mr. Vizetelly has a high opinion of the strength of the various defensive works which protect Charleston harbor, and considers Fort Johnson and Moultrie almost impregnable. The open battery, without casement or adequate traverses, does not, however, impress one with any great idea of power; and we doubt not, when our iron-clads renew the attack, but they will find Fort Sumter and the other works previous to iron argument.*

Vizetelly's next published illustration was a sketch of Confederates sinking torpedoes at night in Charleston Harbor. He noted, "I will be silent as to how many thousand pounds of powder are contained in each of these strange engines of warfare." *Harper's Weekly* again copied this illustration but credited Vizetelly only as "an English artist" and gave no credit to the *Illustrated London News*.

In early 1863, Charleston was insulated from the Federal army. There had been no attempt to seize the city of secession since the disastrous Union defeat at Secessionville in June 1862. Despite the Federal blockade, Southern blockade runners routinely slipped in and out of the city. Fancy dresses, silk, wine and even books were making it to Charleston from England. There

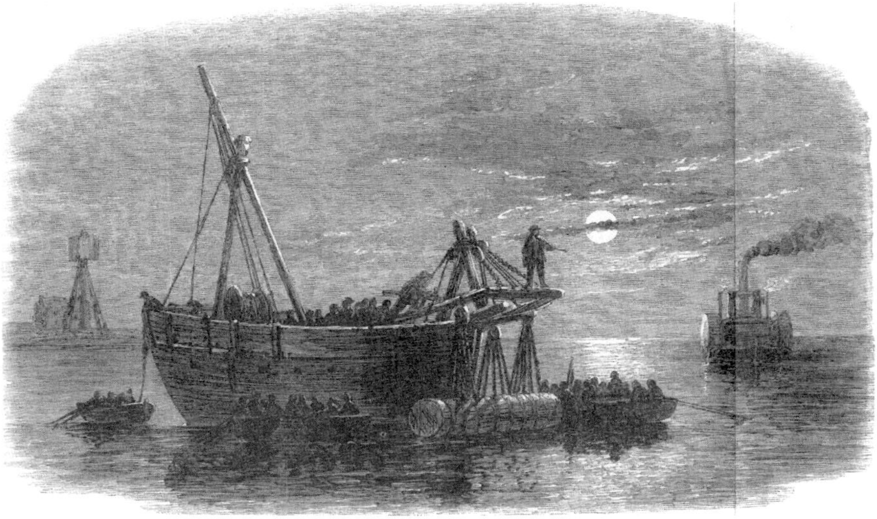

Sinking Confederate torpedoes by moonlight in the shipping channel of Charleston Harbor.

were other amusements in Charleston that pampered the city despite the raging war in Virginia and the West. The city boasted to have "Dr. Cohen's Soda Water Fountain…the only one of its kind running in the Confederacy." An ad in the Charleston newspaper announced that Messieurs Marjenhoff and Bredenberg "have on hand…a large supply of Hamburg Lager Beer."

Though the annual South Carolina Jockey Club race in February 1863 had been cancelled, other social institutions continued to operate. In the spring, the "Grand Ball and Festival," given by the Amicita Club at Hibernian Hall, was still held. The flyers announced that "the services of the Celebrated Palmetto Band have been engaged for the occasion." Vizetelly, never one to miss a social occasion, took advantage of every opportunity.

Vizetelly also forwarded a sketch of the new Confederate ironclads attacking the Union blockading squadron off Charleston. He wrote, "For months the people of Charleston have been busily engaged constructing two iron-clad gun-boats on the same plan as the old *Merrimac*, and within the last few weeks they were completed, and only waited an opportunity to measure their strength with the enemy's fleet blockading the port."

In addition to the scenes of military interest, Vizetelly traveled through the countryside to explore the South Carolina plantations. In March he sketched two images: one of a planter's residence and the second of the planter's family. The reporter's observations were forwarded with the sketches:

Though we are in mid-March here, the climate is most temperate and beautiful, resembling very much the warm sunny June days at home. What the heat will be in the summer time you may readily imagine. After May, however, the planters residing on the river banks remove their families to the "pine barrens," or upper country, the malaria arising from the swamps and rice lands making it dangerous to whites to remain during the hot months in the neighborhood of the river. The trees to the right of the engraving are three of the loftiest palmettos I have yet seen. The dwarf plant at their foot is the aloe, which blooms once or twice in a century.

The second engraving pictured the servants with the planter's children. The paper quoted:

However repugnant slavery as an institution must be to the English mind, no useful purpose is to be gained by keeping the eyes shut to the undoubted

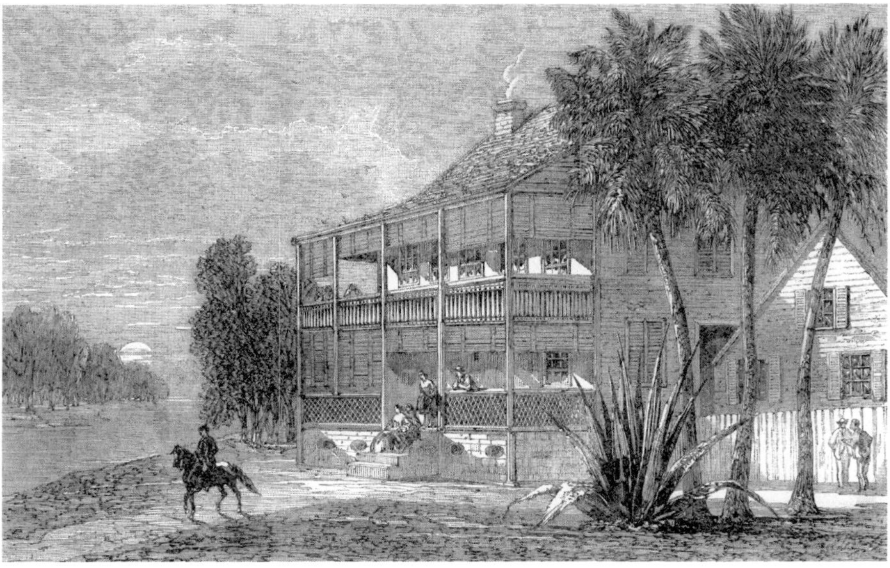

Planter's residence on the Cumbee River, South Carolina.

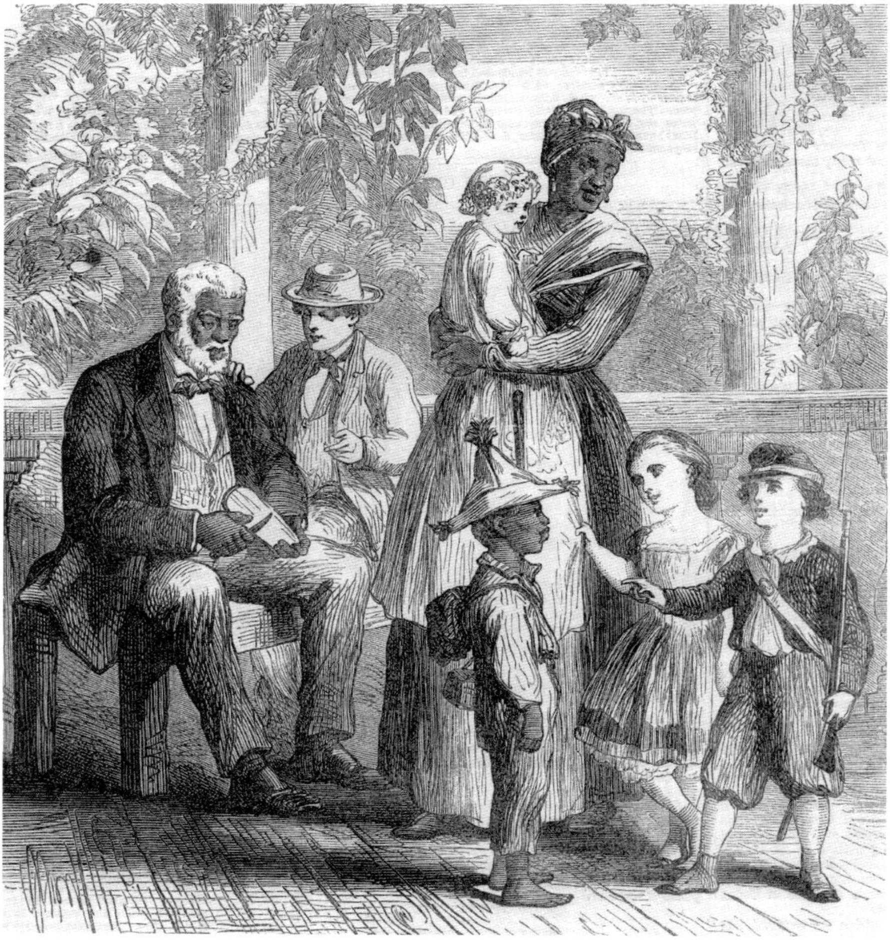

Domestic life on a South Carolina plantation.

> *fact that where slaves are well treated, many of them grow accustomed to, and happy under, their servitude. This becomes easier when it is recollected that the children of the family grow up among the Negro domestic servants, and often learn to regard them with as much affection as they show their own parents.*

Confederate authorities received intelligence that the Union fleet based at Port Royal, South Carolina, would soon attack Savannah. Beauregard went to Savannah to inspect the defenses and invited Vizetelly to join him. He was there to witness the attack on Fort McAllister.

Beauregard soon realized that the Savannah attack was simply a diversion and that the real force of attack was to be on Charleston. On April 5, nine Union ironclads and several steamships appeared just outside the entrance to Charleston Harbor. The next day, twenty-four wooden vessels joined the warships. On April 7, Beauregard was advised that twenty additional ships were in the Stono River south of Charleston.

Vizetelly wrote:

> *I have every faith in the result of the coming encounter, for never at any time have the Confederates been more determined to do or die than they express themselves now. Every preparation has been made, every appliance pressed into service by General Ripley, the Brigadier commanding, to give the foe a warm reception; and, surrounded as he is, apparently by obstacles that appear insurmountable, his zeal and success seem perfectly wonderful. His head-quarters during the coming fight will be in Fort Sumter itself, and, as he expresses it, he will "fight it low down" until not a brick nor stone is left for another to rest upon before he gives in. If the mail-clad monsters now in the offing are repulsed, it will be to General Ripley and the brave men under him that victory will be due.*

Vizetelly felt that the attack by the Union fleet would "assuredly be one of the most extraordinary ever witnessed—armour-plated ships against sand-batteries, earth works, and brick and stone forts." He received permission to establish his position with Ripley at Fort Sumter. At 3:00 p.m. on April 7, Vizetelly boarded a small transport to travel to Fort Sumter. On his way he passed the Battery and was fascinated to see the walls filled with Charlestonians waiting to see the attack. He sketched the scene and wrote that "the ladies of Charleston had no undue fear for the result of the attack, which, if successful, would place their homes at the mercy of an exasperated foe."

The attacking Federal fleet, led by Rear Admiral Samuel F. Du Pont, included the ironclad frigate *New Ironsides*, the double-turret ironclad *Keokuk* and the monitors *Montauk*, *Patapsco*, *Catskill*, *Nantucket*, *Passaic*, *Nahant* and *Weehawken*. The lead monitor, the *Weehawken*, commanded by Captain John Rogers, moved in to challenge Fort Sumter. The Confederate batteries allowed the fleet to move through the shipping channel until they were in a position such that a circle of fire from Morris Island, James Island, Fort Sumter and Sullivan's Island could be unleashed against the ships.

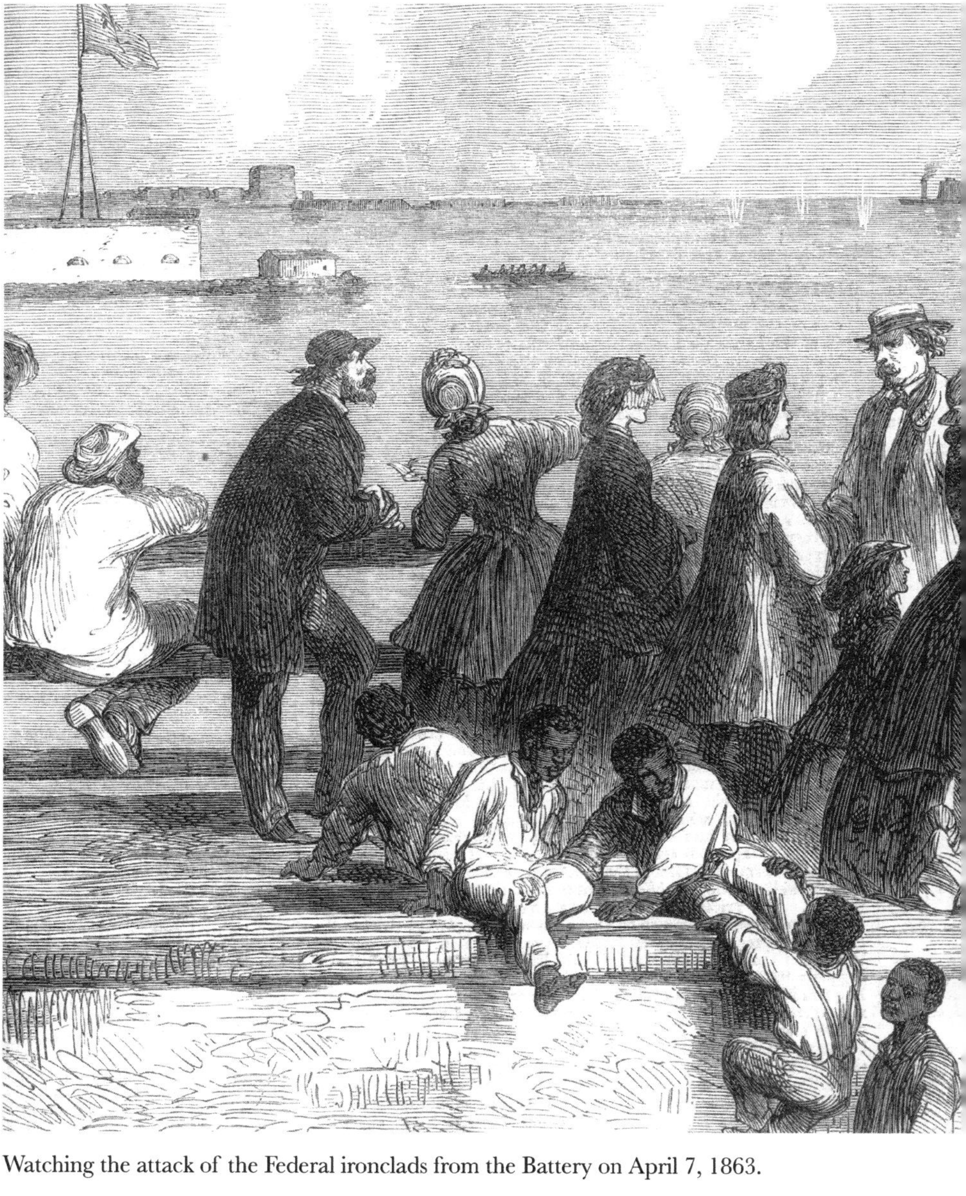

Watching the attack of the Federal ironclads from the Battery on April 7, 1863.

The *Passaic* had to withdraw first after its turret was damaged. Next the *Nahant* retreated after receiving severe damage. The *Keokuk*, though last in formation, steamed ahead to take the closest position to Fort Sumter. After receiving ninety direct hits, the *Keokuk* limped out of formation and anchored off Morris Island to later sink.

Vizetelly reported:

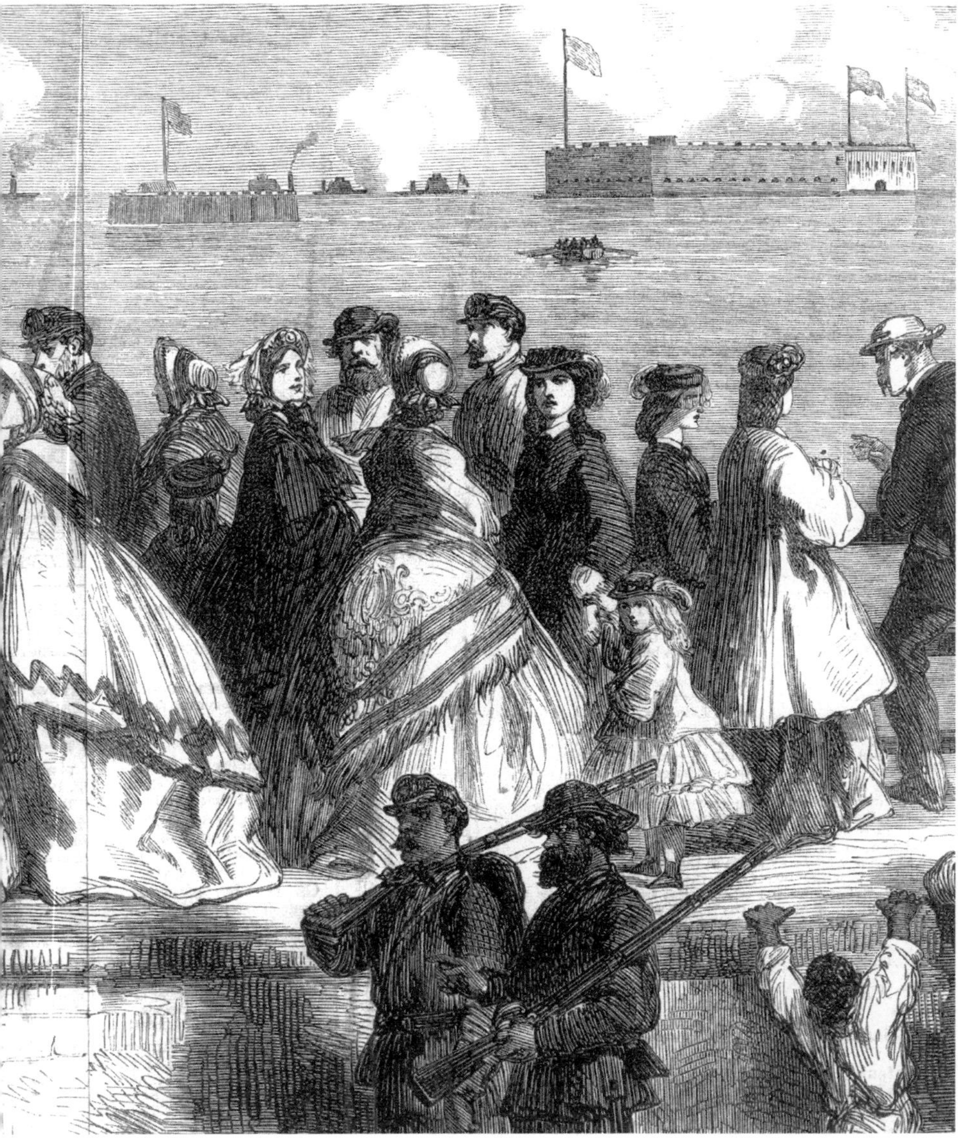

The engagement...lasted two hours and twenty-five minutes...There were eight turreted ironclads, including the boasted double-turreted Keokuk *and an immense plated frigate known as the* Ironsides. *All these marine monsters were armed with eleven and fifteen inch guns. They were all struck by the forts repeatedly; and after maintaining the fight for the time I named, they steamed away, evidently much damaged. This morning we have ample evidence of the fact...Clothes clotted with blood have been picked*

> *up that floated from the* Keokuk, *and there can be little doubt that she was pierced through and through, and that the loss of life on board her has been severe...The Confederate loss does not amount to more than four men killed and about a dozen wounded. There were a few casualties here* [Fort Sumter] *and we had two of our guns dismounted by the fire from the ships. The fight may be renewed at any moment if the Federals have the stomach for the attempt; but I think they have suffered too much to provoke another encounter...The Yankee transports have landed some thousands of men on Folly Island, south of Morris Island, who will, as soon as possible receive every attention.*

Vizetelly sketched a scene that had occurred in Fort Moultrie during the attack:

> *The Sketch I send you illustrates one of the most gallant feats in the bombardment of Fort Charleston. I had left my position in Battery Bee and reached Fort Moultrie just in time to witness it. The action was at its height when a ball cut the flagstaff in tow just above the traverse, and as it fell it struck a poor fellow on the back of the head, killing him on the spot. The*

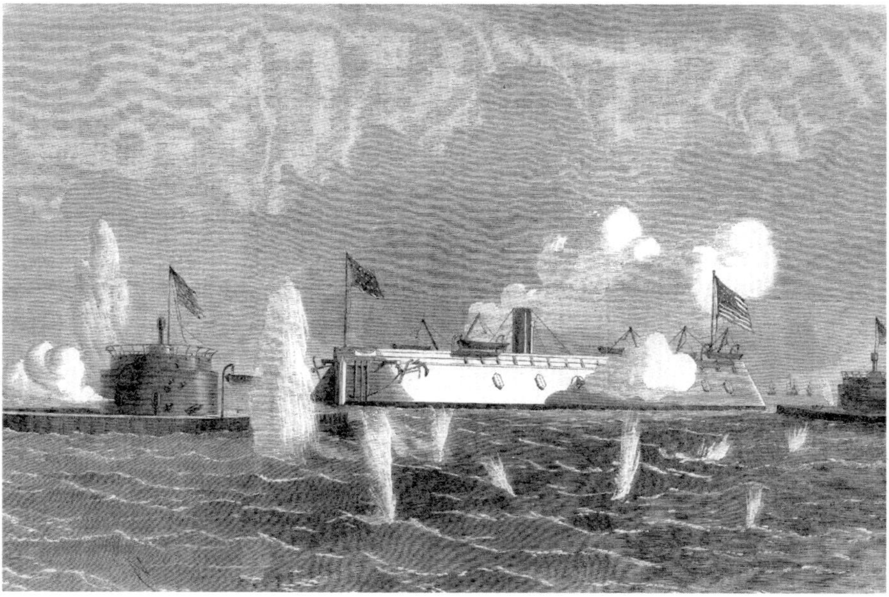

The ironclad frigate *New Ironsides* leading the attack on Fort Sumter.

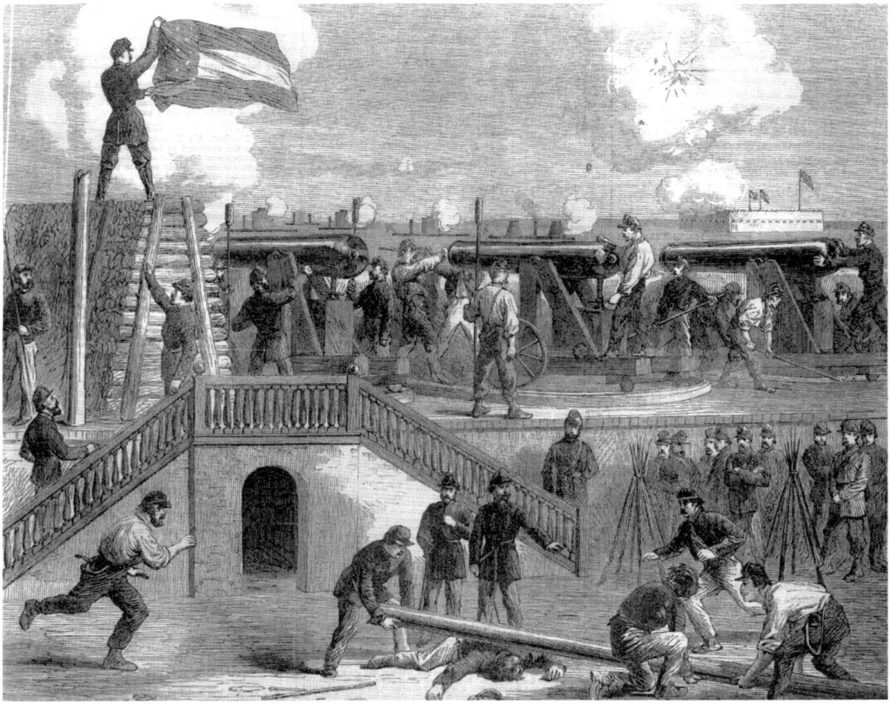

Scene at Fort Moultrie during the Federal attack on Charleston.

quartermaster of the battalion in the fort immediately sprang forward, and seizing the fallen flag tore it from its hold and leapt on to the traverse, where he stood under the heavy fire immovable, until a jurymast was rigged and raised in the place of the shattered staff. The soldiers in the foreground of my Sketch are removing the broken staff from the body of the poor fellow, who lies beneath it, and who was the only man killed by the Federal fire.

Du Pont's bold frontal attack on Fort Sumter was a complete disaster. One seaman aboard the *Catskill* revealed, "Officers and men were astonished to see the injuries done to these supposed invulnerable ironclads." C.W. Whitey, the designer of the *Keokuk*, boldly asserted that his new ironclad featured a shot-proof design. His boasting rang hollow to its crew as the ship suffered nineteen holes during the battle. In total, the Union ironclad fleet fired only 154 rounds in the battle, while the Confederate batteries and Fort Sumter fired 2,209.

That night the work parties at Fort Sumter began repairing the casemates damaged by the attack. Most of the damage was around the embrasures.

Many sandbags were brought in to strengthen the casemates where needed to prepare for a possible renewal of the attack.

The Federal fleet anchored overnight just outside the entrance to Charleston Harbor and withdrew to Port Royal the next day. Du Pont wrote in his report to Washington, "I attempted to take the bull by the horns, but he was too much for us. These monitors are miserable failures where forts are concerned." He was relieved of his command by the summer.

While Vizetelly was in Charleston, Union major general Ulysses S. Grant leading the Army of Tennessee crossed the Mississippi River intending to capture Vicksburg, the last Confederate stronghold on the river. After two assaults in mid-May failed with heavy casualties, Grant decided to lay siege to the city. Confederate lieutenant general John C. Pemberton, commander of the Confederate troops, was trapped, and reinforcements from General Joe Johnston, commander of the Confederate Department of the West, were his only hope.

By the summer, Vizetelly packed his bag for the West, traveling with several regiments ordered to report to General Johnston. Vizetelly wrote of his experience traveling:

> *The campaign in the valley of Mississippi will, I believe, decide the duration of the war; and the battles fought there, under the respective leaderships of General Johnston and General Grant (Federal), will, I think, be on a much larger scale than those in Virginia.*
>
> *The incident illustrated in the Engraving will give you an idea of the perils of traveling on a used-up military railroad. Three times the cars ran off line, injuring many of the men; and on one of those occasions the carriage in which I was got smashed all to pieces, and for some time I was unaware of what had taken place until I shook myself together, and then I found that my arm was badly bruised.*
>
> *We can hear heavy firing in the direction of Vicksburg. The place still holds out bravely, with a loss altogether, so says a prisoner, of nearly 20,000 men. The dead are lying unburied between the besieged and the besiegers. The town is completely invested, and we only get intelligence by the occasional courier, who runs the gauntlet of the Union lines.*

Vizetelly reached Jackson, Mississippi, forty miles from Vicksburg, and did join Johnston's army. He witnessed the reoccupation of Jackson by the Confederates:

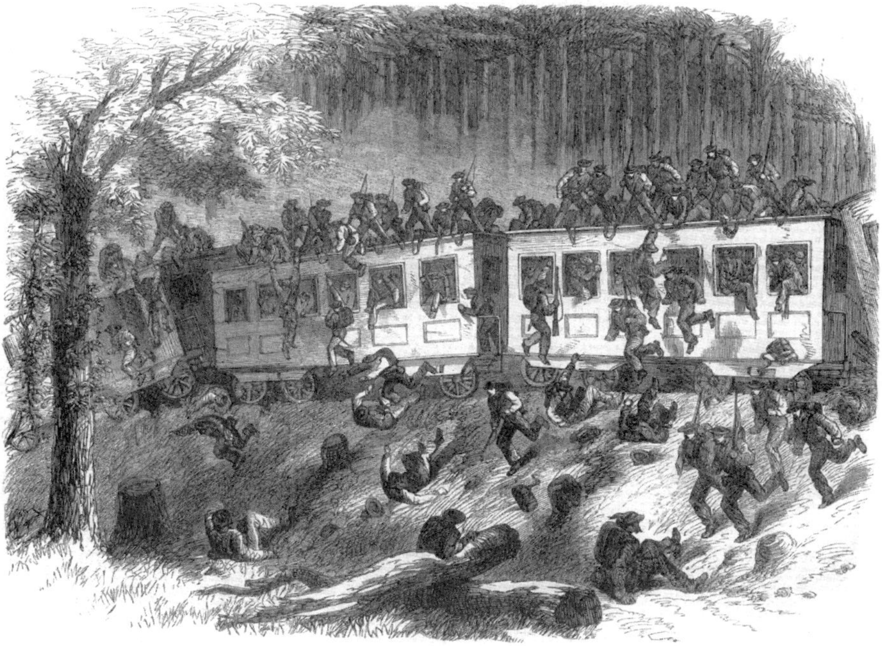

Train with reinforcements for General Johnston running off the tracks in the forests of Mississippi.

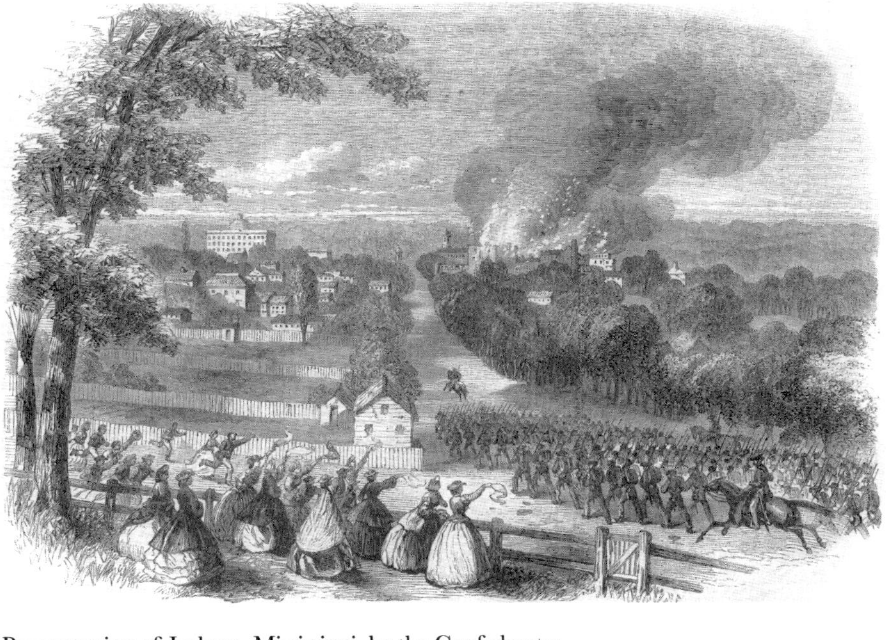

Reoccupation of Jackson, Mississippi, by the Confederates.

Jackson for a short time was occupied by the Federal army under General Grant. The enemy entered the town in overwhelming force after a smart engagement with very inferior numbers, who were compelled to retire on the army collecting under General Johnston for the relief of Vicksburg. During the occupation, which lasted two days, the Yankees were guilty of every kind of vandalism; they sacked houses, stole clothing from the negroes, burst open their trunks, and took what little money they had, besides which they drove off the stoutest and strongest, against their will, to work on the intrenchments; and behaved, indeed, more like savages than civilized troops. I arrived here the day before yesterday with the reinforcements, a portion of which you see entering the town. I entered it with them. We found the place in flames, being fired indiscriminately by a retreating army, who fled precipitately before our advance.

The country for forty miles round Vicksburg is covered with small encampments of women and children who have been driven from their homes by predatory bands of Northern soldiers. Ladies who have been reared in luxury are now reduced to the discomforts and hardships of a bivouac, which they bear uncomplainingly, being willing to suffer in a cause for which their husbands, lovers, and brothers are fighting. With nothing but a few yards of canvas to protect them from the frequent thunderstorms which burst in terrific magnificence at this season of the year over Mississippi, they support with dignity their heavy trial. A cavalry officer has just come into the camp with letters and has given animation to the Illustration.

During the siege, the Confederates and civilians in Vicksburg lost most communication with the outside. Scurvy, malaria, dysentery and diarrhea were ravaging the population. Men in Johnston's army volunteered to run the Union lines to get munitions and what food they could carry into the city. Vizetelly reported one such attempt to resupply Vicksburg:

It had been reported to General Johnston that the troops in the beleaguered city were beginning to run shot of caps, the frequent assaults of the enemy upon the trenches having necessitated a continuous fire from the garrison, which had much reduced the stock. Volunteers were immediately called for to carry in a fresh supply; and of the first twelve who made the attempt every one of them was either captured or shot. Subsequently, however, numbers succeeded in getting into the town, and even returning to our camps; and of the party illustrated in my sketch all were fortunate enough to evade the

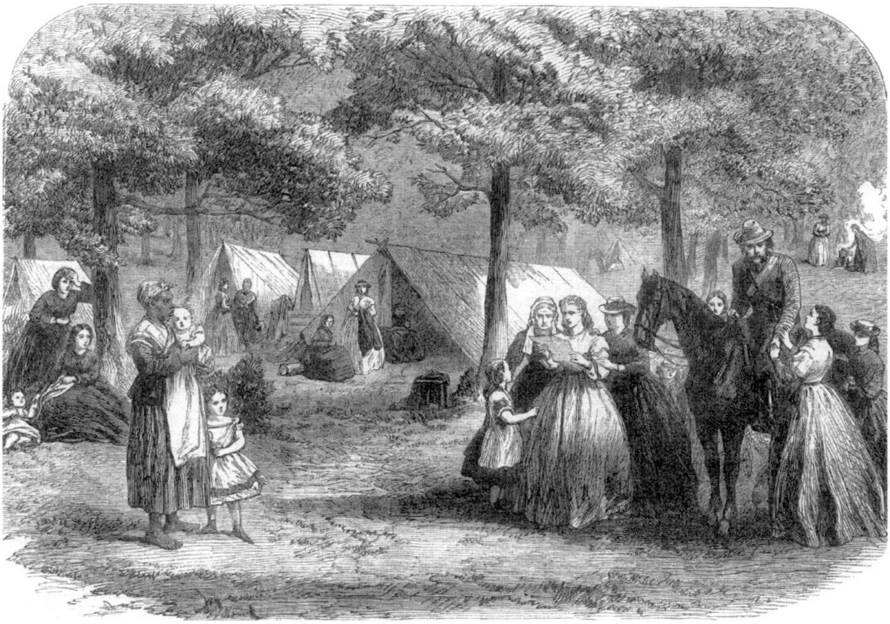

Southern refugees encamping in the woods near Vicksburg.

> *vigilance of the Yankee guards. I accompanied them some distance on the way, and saw them enter the ravines and gorges at the outer line of Federal pickets. This was at a point some twelve miles from Vicksburg; and as I lay on the ground in the calm, quiet night I could distinctly hear sounds of musketry between the loud booming of the mortars. Probably a sortie was taking place, Confederates having made one or two at that time which were brilliantly successful. These scouts lay in the woods during the day, and when night came they crept on their hands and knees through successive lines of the enemy's pickets, choosing the roughest paths and taking advantage of the ravines…crawling along in the dense shadows avoiding every gleam of moonlight, and prepared at any moment to use the revolver or the knife.*

Pemberton, on July 3, finally sent a note to Grant that he was prepared to surrender Vicksburg. The surrender was made official on July 4, a day selected by Pemberton hoping for favorable terms. The Confederates surrendered 29,495 men, 172 cannons and 50,000 rifles, critical resources that the South could ill afford to lose. Not wanting to expend the resources to transfer so many captives to prison, the Confederates were paroled and released by Grant.

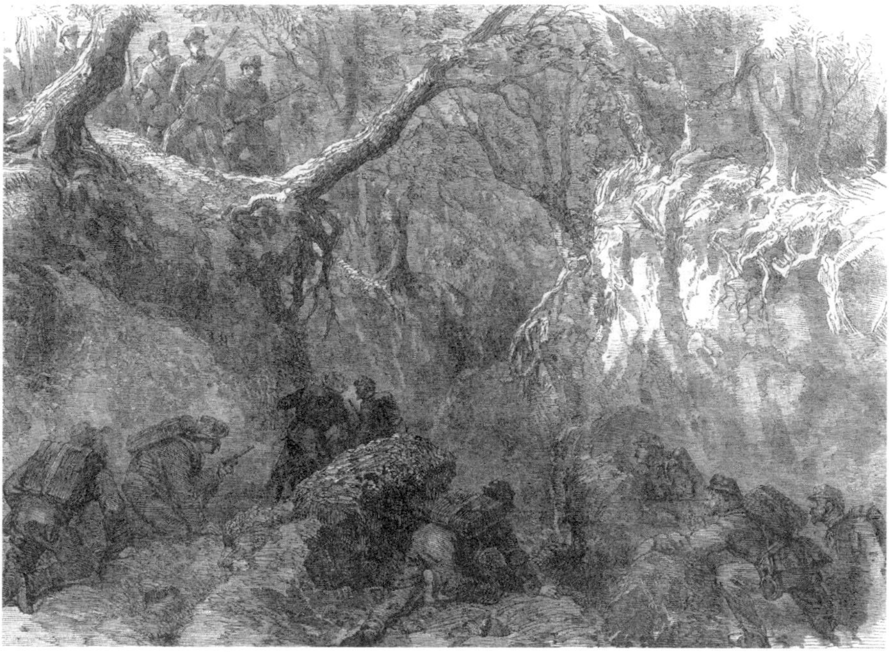

Confederate scouts running through the Federal pickets to resupply the garrison at Vicksburg.

After the fall of Vicksburg, Vizetelly decided to return to Charleston. Union general Quincy A. Gillmore had been given command of the Department of the South on June 12. One of his first acts was to replace Admiral Du Pont with Admiral John A. Dahlgren. Gillmore and Dahlgren then turned their attention to Charleston, the "head of the snake" as far as the North was concerned. Gillmore determined that the first stage of seizing control of the harbor was to take Battery Wagner, a sand fortification on Morris Island.

Suffering through myriad inconveniences and delays, Vizetelly did not reach Charleston until July 15. He had already missed the Union army landing 3,800 troops on James Island, though this was just a diversion and a probing attack on Battery Wagner on July 11. He once again took a room at the Charleston Hotel and found himself in the company of two other Europeans: Captain Fitzgerald Ross, an Englishman serving in the Austrian army assigned as an observer in America, and Captain Justus Scheibert, a German who enlisted in the Confederate army for active duty.

The three Europeans spent several days dining and drinking, enjoying the company of others from the Old World. Their idle time was woefully short, however, as the Union army was already maintaining a daily barrage of artillery from land batteries and the fleet trying to soften the Confederate positions on Morris Island.

At 10:00 a.m. on July 18, the Union batteries opened fire on Battery Wagner. Shortly, the Union fleet joined in and the combined land and sea artillery was firing upon the sand battery no less than fourteen shells per minute. At 5:00 p.m., all Union guns were ordered to fire as rapidly as possible. At dusk, after ten hours of constant bombardment, Gillmore was ready for his frontal assault on Battery Wagner by his infantry. One Union soldier wrote, "No one would suppose that a human being, or a bird even, could live for a moment upon that fort." Vizetelly observed that the bombardment "from ordnance of hitherto unheard-of caliber would have demoralized or driven the garrison out."

Gillmore organized the attack in three brigades and assumed that his army could simply overwhelm the Confederate battery. By this time of day the tide was high, leaving only a narrow beach accessible for the attack. Vizetelly observed the attack, writing:

> [They] *could have not had less that 8000 men engaged, some of whom reached the parapet and died there; yet, with only 1500 to oppose them, they were eventually driven back with a loss equal to the entire force of the Confederates in the fort. The period chosen for my illustration is the moment when the last shell fired from the fleet bursts over the battery; and the troops, illumined by the glare, are seen rushing to the parapet to repel the assault. Some of the enemy have already reached the crest of the work, but only to pay for their temerity by falling where they stand.*
>
> *All through the night we could hear the screams and groans of the wounded lying within a few yards of us; but as a continual fire was kept up by the advanced pickets it was impossible to do anything for them without running great risk of being shot. Early in the morning, however, the Federals sent a flag of truce, asking for a cessation of hostilities, that they might bury their dead. The first demand was granted, but they were told they could not be permitted to come within the lines of the Confederates and the latter would perform the last offices for the fallen enemy. In the ditch they lay piled, Negroes and whites, four and five deep on each other; there could not have been less than 250 in the moat, some partially submerged; and altogether over 600 were buried by the Southerners.*

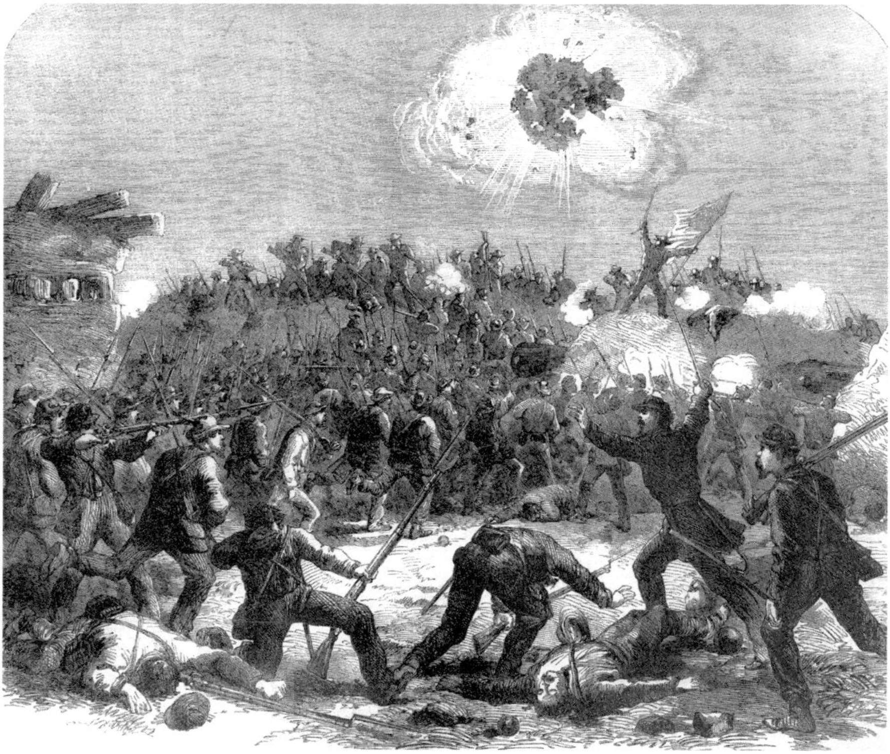

Assault on Fort Wagner on the night of July 18.

In short, the attack on Battery Wagner was a catastrophe for the Union army. Union casualties totaled 1,515 compared to only 174 for the Confederates.

Unable to take Battery Wagner, Gillmore regrouped and strengthened his positions on Folly Island and the southern tip of Morris Island. Believing that if he could fire directly upon Charleston he could weaken the resolve of the citizens and General Beauregard, Gillmore ordered Colonel Serrell to find a place between Morris Island and James Island to establish such a battery.

Serrell tested many marsh locations, finding the mud as deep as twelve feet deep in some places. Finally, he designed a gun platform that would "float" on the marsh. Building the parapet was an ordeal itself, requiring the transportation of thirteen thousand sandbags weighing more than eight hundred tons across a causeway built of wooden planks 1,700 feet long. One Union engineer remarked, "We're building a pulpit on which

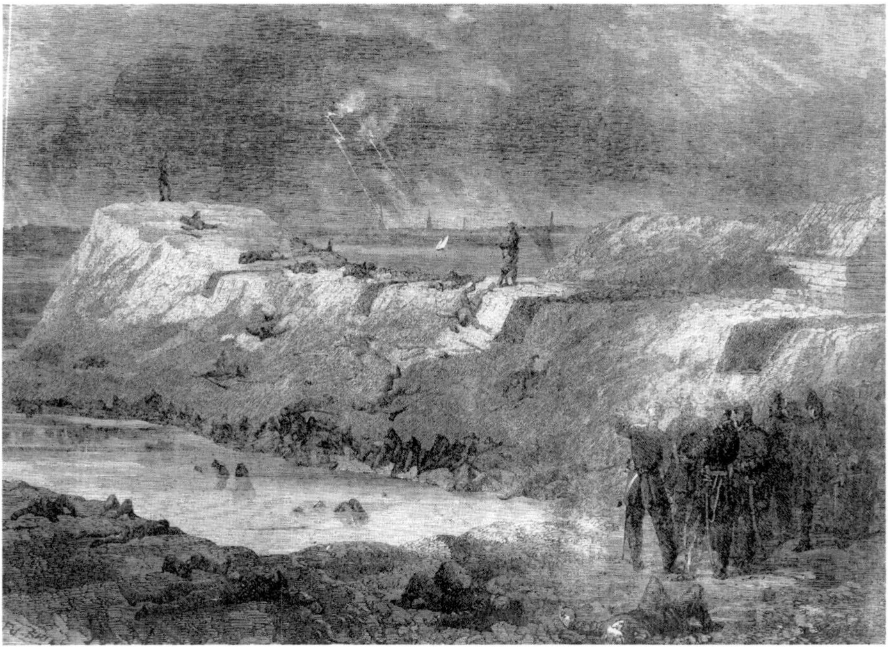

The southern slope of the ditch surrounding Fort Wagner the morning after the attack.

a Swamp Angel will preach." The nickname Swamp Angel stuck for the battery being constructed.

In order to fire a shell 7,900 yards to reach the city of Charleston, Union engineers calculated that the eight-inch Parrott gun would have to be elevated to an angle never before used. On the night of August 21, Vizetelly settled into his hotel room reading about the Battle of Waterloo. Crossing into the hours past midnight, he was lying awake in his bed when the Swamp Angel fired the first shot at 1:30 a.m. on August 22. He described the shot as resembling "the whirr of a phantom brigade of cavalry in mid-air."

An intense explosion threw him toward the window. Looking out, he could see smoke and fire in the building across the street. Knowing that never before had a shell traveled the distance between the city and the Union positions, he considered that "a high meteor had fallen." Minutes later, a second shot was fired into the city nearby.

Running downstairs to the lobby, Vizetelly encountered "terrified gentlemen" who had traveled to Charleston to purchase black market goods referred to as "blockade cargoes." He observed that they rushed about "in the scantiest of costumes and the wildest alarms."

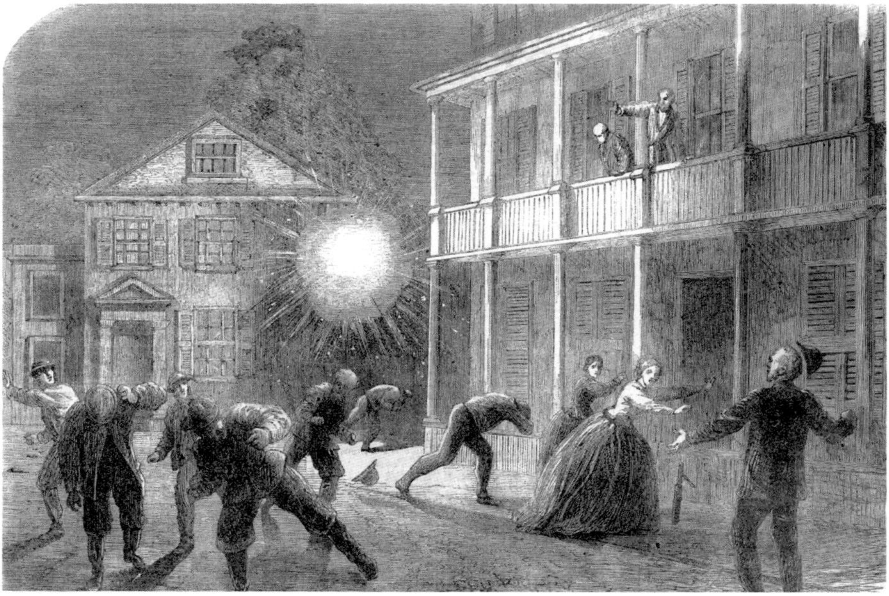

The Union army firing into downtown Charleston.

Vizetelly wrote of that night:

> *One perspiring individual of portly dimensions was trotting to and fro with one boot on and the other in his hand, and this was nearly all the dress he could boast of. In his excitement and terror he had forgotten the number of his room from which he has hastened at the first alarm, and his distress was ludicrous to behold. Another, in a semi-state of nudity with a portion of his garments on his arm, barked the shins of every one in his way in his efforts to drag an enormous trunk to the staircase. On reaching the hall I found a motley crowd, some of whom with the biggest of words were cursing the Federal commanders. Whirr! Came another shell over the roof, and down on their faces went every man of them into tobacco-juice and cigar-ends and clattering among the spittoons. I need not say that this is a class of men from whom the Confederacy hopes nothing; on the contrary, by their extortion, practiced on a suffering people, they have made themselves execrated. If a shell could have fallen in their midst and exterminated the whole race of hucksters, it would have been of great benefit to the South.*
>
> *The population was now aroused, the streets filled with women and children making their way to the upper part of the city, where they would*

find comparative safety. The volunteer fire-brigades brought out their engines, and parties of the citizen reserves were organized rapidly and quietly, to be in readiness to give assistance where required. The first engine that reached the house struck by the first shell was one belonging to a Negro company, and at it they went with a will, subduing the fire in a marvelously short time. At every successive whirr about them the niggers shouted quaint invectives against "cussed bobolitionists," scattering for shelter until the danger was passed. Through the streets I went, and down to the Battery promenade, meeting on my way sick and bed-ridden people carried from their homes on mattresses, and mothers with infants in their arms running they knew not whither. Reaching the promenade, I cast my eyes towards the Federal position, and presently beyond James Island, across a marsh that separates it from Morris Island, came a flash, then a dull report and, after an interval of some seconds, a frightful rushing sound above me told the path the shell had taken; its flight must have been five miles!

During the bombardment, Vizetelly met his friends Captain Scheibert and Captain Ross in the hotel bar. The three Europeans passed the time by placing bets on the next landing location of each successive Federal shell. Captain Ross would write of their ludicrous game in which he offered Vizetelly "a thousand to one that a shell we heard coming would not hit either of us." The English reporter accepted the bet, "forgetting that if he won he would have had but a small chance of realizing his wager—and, of course, I won my dollar."

After two hours of constant shelling, the firing slowed and near dawn stopped. During the long night, ten incendiary and six explosive shells were fired into Charleston. Exhausted, Vizetelly and many of the other guests at the hotel went to bed. That morning, English, French and Spanish consuls that were stationed in Charleston traveled under a flag of truce to meet with General Gillmore. They vehemently objected to the firing on innocent women and children in Charleston. Gillmore indicated that the shelling would continue, but he would give anyone left in Charleston the next twenty-four hours to clear the city.

Many people left Charleston to join friends or families at plantations in the country parishes. As Vizetelly reported, "There were hundreds whose circumstances compelled them to remain."

The next day, the firing from the Swamp Angel continued as promised by Gillmore. Finally, upon the thirty-sixth shot fired from the elevated Parrott gun, the barrel could no longer withstand the pressure, and the Swamp Angel burst.

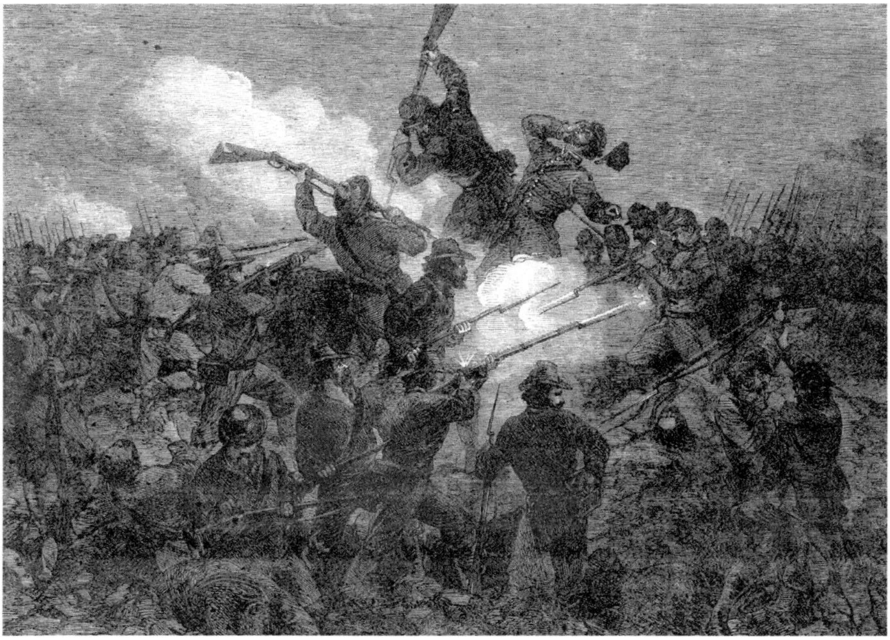

The fight in front of the rifle-pits at Fort Wagner.

After the firing ceased, Vizetelly wrote:

> *It was now that, foiled at all points and smarting under his failures, the Federal general was guilty of that barbarity which has disgraced him as a soldier. Unable to capture the forts…he intimated that unless they were surrendered, he would turn his powerful guns upon the city. The threat was disregarded—disbelieved in, no doubt…in violation of warfare, he turned his guns on unoffending women and children.*

Battery Wagner had proven to be a formidable defensive position, but after the July attack several additional defensive features were added. South of the fort, the Confederates spread several types of torpedoes (land mines) hidden in the sand to discourage the enemy from advancing on the fort. Still farther south of the mines, the Confederates established a series of rifle pits where troops were stationed to fire upon any approaching enemy.

The Federal army had been occupied digging a series of zigzag trenches that approached the Confederate rifle pits. On August 26, the Twenty-fourth Massachusetts prepared to attack. Each man was issued extra ammunition

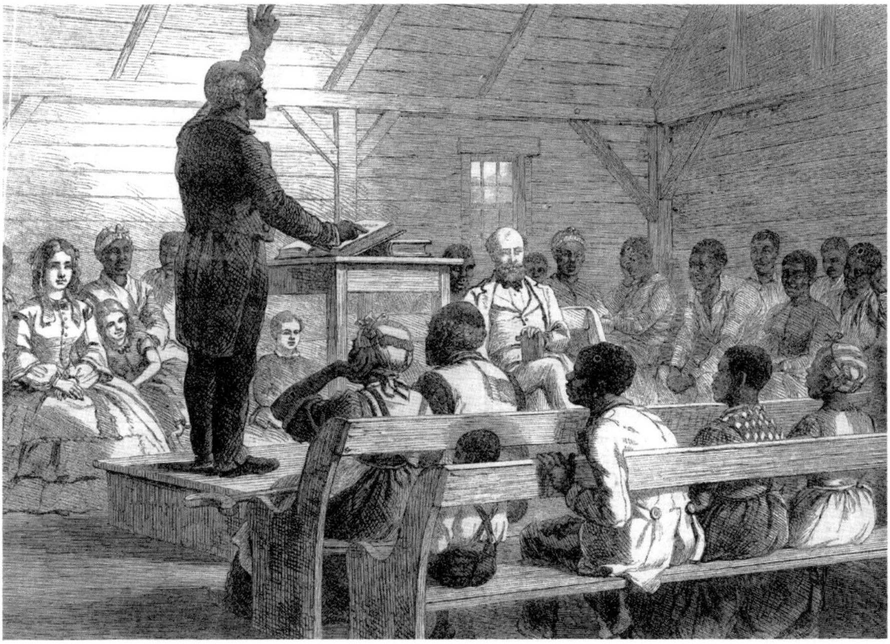

Family worship on a plantation in South Carolina.

and a shovel to dig in his position if needed. At 6:30 p.m., the Massachusetts Volunteers, supported by the Third New Hampshire Volunteers, attacked the rifle pits, overwhelming the eighty-six men of the Sixty-first North Carolina. From the protection of Battery Wagner, Vizetelly sketched the skirmish.

Sensing a stalemate in the action at Charleston, Vizetelly made plans to travel to Tennessee. Before he departed, he made a sketch of a worship service of a South Carolina plantation:

> *The "incumbent" was an intelligent old house servant, a slave. He could read, but not write; and his extempore sermons, although sometimes marred by his predilection for high-sounding phrases and long words (not always appropriate), were characterized by strong good sense and a certain rude native eloquence, often rising to the dignity of pathos, and admirable adapted to the comprehension and temperament of his audience. The Methodist persuasion is the one which finds most favour among the slaves in the Southern as well as among the free Negroes in the Northern States.*

Chapter 11

CAPTAIN VIZETELLY

On September 14, Vizetelly, Captain Ross and Captain Byrne, another Englishman, left Charleston and traveled to Atlanta and on to north Georgia. As they arrived, they met the first of Longstreet's corps en route to reinforce Braxton Bragg.

While traveling through north Georgia, Vizetelly was invited to travel with a company of Confederate sharpshooters, armed with Whitworth telescopic rifles, firing upon a Federal supply train on Racoon Mountain along the Tennessee River:

> *Since the Federal army has sought refuge in its intrenchments at Chattanooga the object of the Confederates has been to disturb its communications, and if possible to break up its supply trains...The position chosen* [for this sketch] *was twelve miles in rear of the enemy's works, and, unfortunately for them, was not guarded. At the invitation of Captain Gorree, who was to take charge of the party, I accompanied the expedition; and the only way of reaching the place and avoiding the Federal scouts was by taking the Indian trails through the forest heights.*
>
> *Scarcely had we arrived at our destination and got the men hidden behind the rocks, when, far up the gorge, could be heard distinctly the rumbling of approaching wheels. Presently emerged the leading files of an infantry escort, followed by the first waggon. The order was not to fire until the open space of the road in front of us was filled. At last came word, and a score of sharp cracks leapt in with their riders, went down, creating the most dire confusion. Then came a stampede as was never before seen. The teams in front endeavored to gallop on, but were prevented by one or more mules hanging dead in the traces; others behind made an effort to turn, but got blocked by those in the rear. Crack! Crack! still went the rifles, until the road*

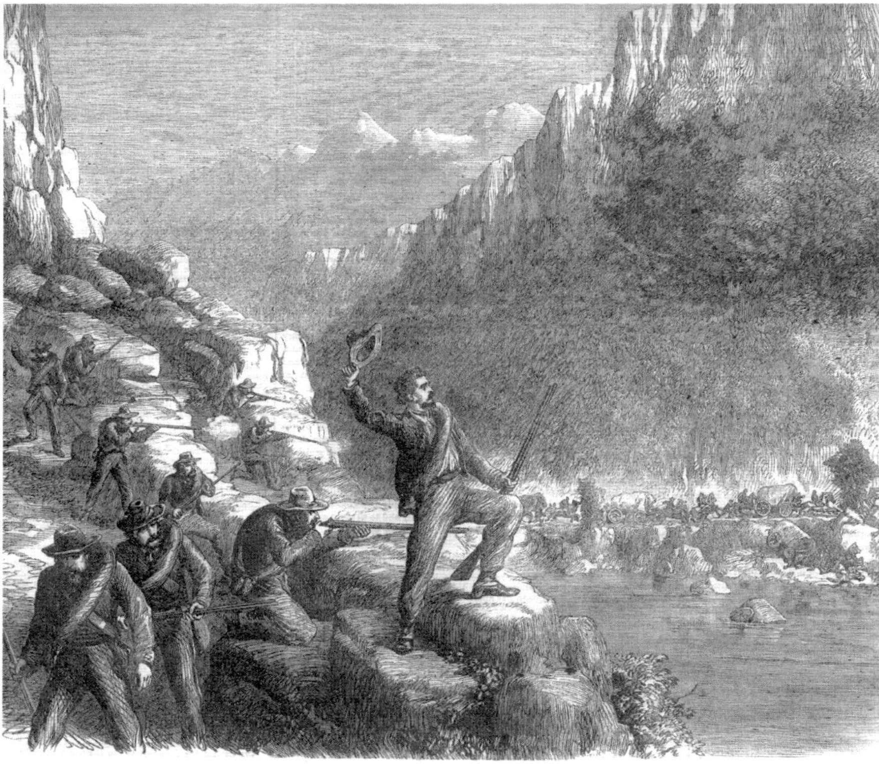

Confederate sharpshooters firing at a Federal supply train on Racoon Mountain on the Tennessee River.

> *was choked with dead and dying men and mules, and overturned waggons. The escort, after firing a few shots in return, fled panic-stricken, followed by the exulting shouts of the Confederate riflemen.*

After a successful campaign through Tennessee in the summer, Union general William Rosencrans and three corps totaling sixty thousand men moved to force the Confederates out of Chattanooga. In mid-September, Confederate commander Braxton Bragg marched back to attack Rosencrans and reoccupy Chattanooga. The Battle of Chickamauga, the most significant Union defeat in the West, was fought on September 19–20.

Vizetelly sketched several views of the layout of the two armies as the battlefield was set:

> *In this view the exact positions of Chattanooga and General Rosencranz's* [sic] *army are, I think, tolerably well defined, the town and camps of the Federalists lying in a bend of the Tennessee river, which here forms the letter U. By drawing a curved line across the superior portion of the letter you have the defensive line of works thrown up by the Northern Commander, and will thus see that this is a position of great strength from the fact that his forces are concentrated in a small space, his left and right resting on each bend of the river. The Confederate lines run from the river at the base of Lookout Mountain, extending along Missionary Ridge, and terminating again on the river to the extreme right, the Federals having the inner side of an arc, and the Confederate the outer. Missionary Ridge is formed by the range of hills running from the right across the middle distance, and from amidst the foliage may be seen peeping here and there the sparse tents of the Southern army. Beyond, still to the right, are the lofty peaks of the Unaka Mountains, forming a portion of the Alleghany chain, and the whole scene of valley and distant purple hills, with the cloud shadows sobering the rich tints that sparkle in the golden autumn sunshine, make up a landscape that requires no further assistance of nature to make it perfect.*

Vizetelly wrote of the battle:

> *The Battle of Chickamauga, of which your readers will doubtless have heard long before this sketch can reach you, was one of the most brilliant victories ever gained by the South, though, unfortunately, not decisive in its results, for, owing to the incompetency or apathy of the confederate Commander-in-Chief* [Braxton Bragg], *the Federal General was allowed to collect his scattered columns behind the intrenchments of Chattanooga. The fight commenced on the 19th of September, and fluctuated throughout the day with varying chances, both armies occupying their respective positions when darkness put a stop to the conflict. At twelve o'clock on that night General Longstreet, to the delight of every one, arrived on the field from Virginia, and immediately assumed command of the Confederate left wing, consisting of his own corps of tried veterans from banks of the Rappahannock and Potomac, and Buckner's division from the army of East Tennessee.*
>
> *On the morning of the 20th the battle was renewed, General Longstreet sweeping everywhere from his front the right of the Federal host, crushing them back before the advance of his victorious brigade…You will recollect that General Hood was severely wounded in the arm at Gettysburg, and*

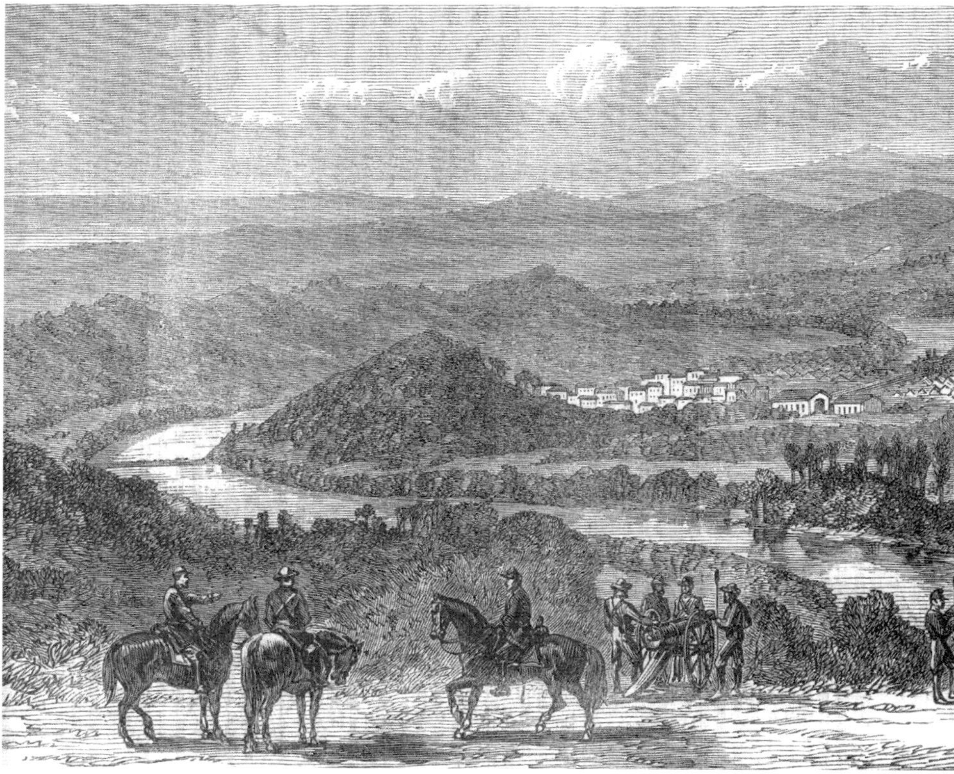

View of Chattanooga and Federal lines from Lookout Mountain.

though still suffering, and compelled to carry the injured limb in a sling, he accompanied his glorious division to the banks of the Tennessee. General Hood is, to my mind, the Bayard of the Confederate Army, literally san peur et sans reproche, *and those who have seen him, as I have seen him at Fredericksburg and elsewhere, at the head of his gallant Texans, will admit I eulogize him no more than he deserves. About two o'clock on the 20th General Hood found his division in front of an opening in the woods, which ascended abruptly for some three or four hundred yards to a most formidable Yankee position on the skirt of a dense piece of forest. Fallen timber served to make its natural strength much stronger, and behind this fortification of logs were posted large bodies of Federal infantry and numerous pieces of artillery. General Hood determined at once to carry the position by assault, and forming his men in two lines, gave the order to advance. The leading column moved forward half way across the opening, under a most withering*

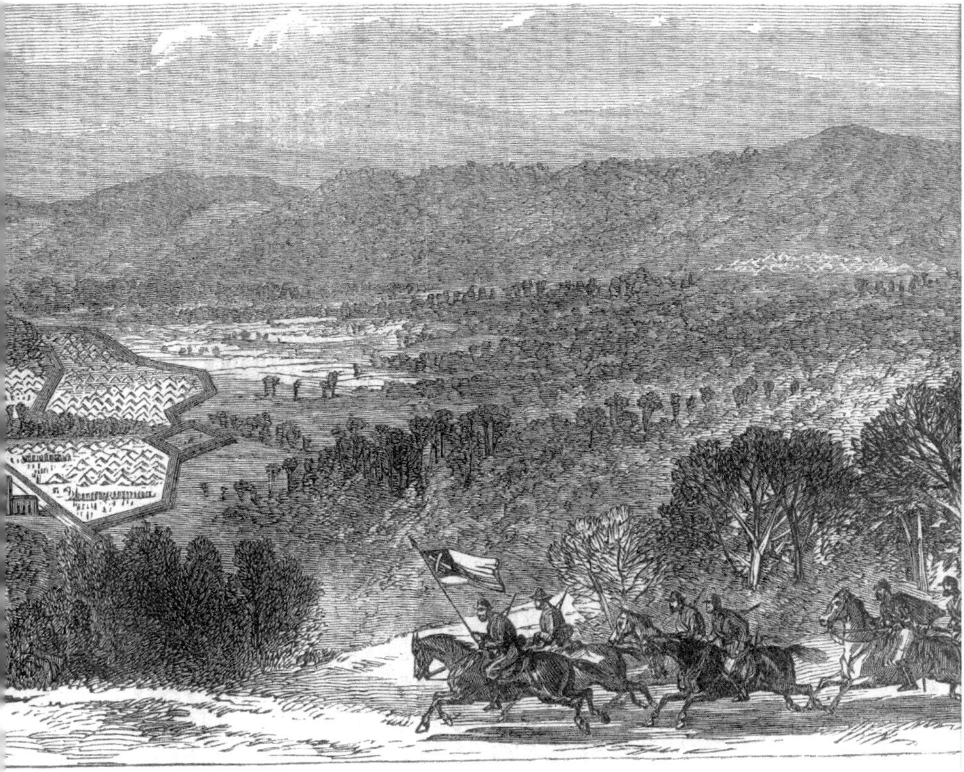

fire, then paused for an instant and discharges their rifles, rushing on, with the bayonet, through the smoke. At this moment General Hood was cheering forward the second column when an Enfield ball passed through his right thigh, smashing the bone to pieces, and as he was removed from the field he heard the shouts of his soldiers proclaiming their success and his revenge.

Having defeated the Federal army, Bragg missed several opportunities to prevent the escape of his enemy. The next day, Rosencrans withdrew to Chattanooga and established a strong defensive position. Infuriated, Confederate general Nathan Bedford Forrest yelled "You are a coward!" to Bragg, his commander.

During the battle, Confederate couriers were being picked off by Union sharpshooters at an alarming rate. A gifted horseman, Vizetelly rode with several messages from General Longstreet to the front lines. After the fighting had subsided, Longstreet commissioned Vizetelly as an "honorary captain" in the Confederate army.

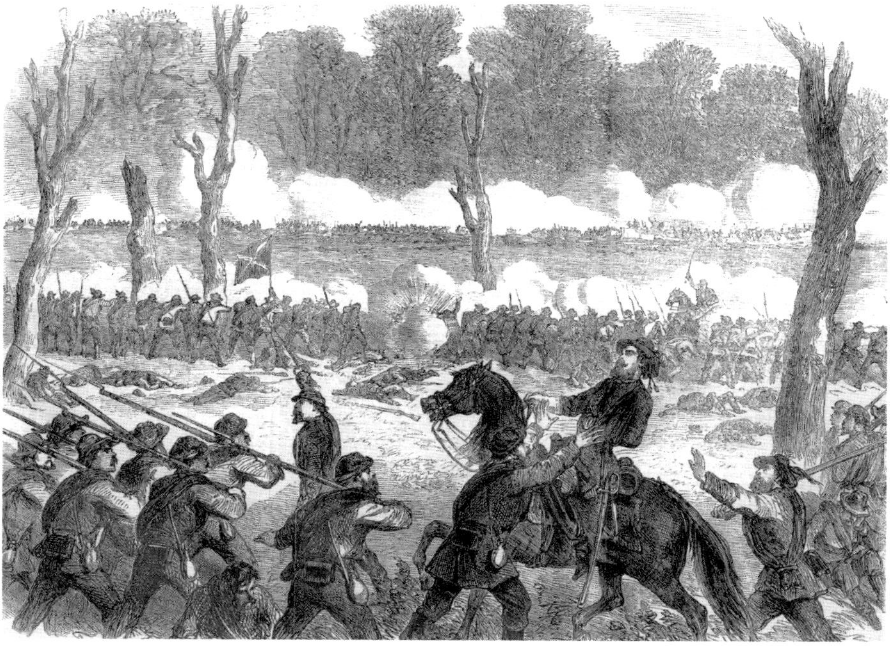

The wounding of General Hood at the Battle of Chickamauga.

After the battle, President Jefferson Davis visited his troops to offer his thanks and congratulations. Vizetelly and his traveling companion Ross were able to meet with Davis. At the Confederate headquarters "there was a good deal of merry-making, and it was no uncommon thing to see half-dozen officers, late at night, dancing *The Perfect Cure*, which was one of the favorite songs of the days in London music halls, and was introduced to our notice by Vizetelly."

On October 22, Vizetelly and Captain Ross left Chattanooga to return to Charleston. During the trip, they spent a week relaxing in Augusta, Georgia. In Charleston, they took their rooms, once again, at the Charleston Hotel. Their Lowcountry friends were delighted to see the return of their affable English compatriots, and many dinners and parties were held in their honor. At one dinner, Vizetelly met the Confederate poet Henry Timrod.

Vizetelly left Charleston accompanied by his countryman Captain Ross to reach Virginia via Wilmington. In Richmond, they checked into the Ballard House, a "modern" four-story hotel on Franklin Street.

Once again, Vizetelly immersed himself in the wartime social life of the city. One Richmond socialite, Mrs. Burton Harrison, wrote of Vizetelly, describing him as "a big, florid, red-bearded Bohemian, of a type totally unfamiliar to us Virginians, who could and would do anything to entertain a circle. In our theatricals…he was a treasure-trove…He painted our scenery and faces, made wigs and armor…sang songs, told stories, danced *pas seuls*, and was generally most kind and amusing."

While the Confederacy was short of some provisions, it seemed that Richmond was not short on food and drink. Vizetelly and Ross entertained a group of friends at the Oriental Saloon. The dinner included "venison, game birds, Madeira, claret, and Havana cigars—all for $631.50 in inflated Confederate currency."

As Christmas neared, Vizetelly and Ross were invited by General J.E.B. Stuart to spend the holiday with him at the headquarters of the Army of Northern Virginia at Orange Courthouse, seventy-three miles northwest of Richmond. It was a bitterly cold winter, but the two Englishmen enjoyed the opportunity to visit their good friend Stuart. Ross would write of the visit: "Vizetelly, who is a great favorite of the General's, told some of his best stories." Several days after their arrival, Robert E. Lee joined them in Orange.

After the holidays, Vizetelly returned to Richmond. In January, he visited the camp of Federal prisoners at Belle Isle. The bridge in the illustration is known as the Petersburg Bridge which connects the Southern Railroad with Richmond. He reported:

> *For some time the cartel regulating the exchange of prisoners between the North and South has been in abeyance, the Federal and Confederate commissioners being at issue on a point of objection raised by the Lincoln Administration. The result of this misunderstanding has been a large increase of the captives on each side, and in Richmond especially the prisons are full to overflowing. In fact, those buildings originally set aside for the accommodation of prisoners of war in the Confederate capital have been found insufficient for the purpose, and the authorities, to provide a remedy, have established a camp of detenus on Belle Isle. This is the largest of the numerous islands that intersect the channel of the James River, in the immediate neighborhood of Richmond, and is well adapted for the purpose to which it has been destined. A swift and turbulent current separates it from either shore, and bold, indeed, would be the swimmer who would risk himself amidst the eddies that hiss and boil on their way to the deeps below. Besides, its position allows of a cordon of sentries around*

its entire circumferences, and these are within challenging distance of each other, making it impossible to pass through them unperceived. In addition to this, the camp occupied by the prisoners is intrenched [sic], *and then there is an inner line of guards pacing around its outskirts, with imperative orders to shoot the first man who attempts to cross the embankment. On a commanding eminence close at hand is a detachment of artillerymen, with a shotted gun frowning on the tents beneath, and at the first sign of an outbreak the iron messengers of death would plough their way through the confused mass of insubordinates. Again, on each bank of the river, there are guns, placed in a position to enfilade the island, and they are kept in readiness for any emergency that may arise.*

When I visited Belle Isle, at the latter end of January, there were more than 7000 prisoners in the camp, all of whom were rank and file from the Federal armies of Virginia and Tennessee. The officers are confined in the "Libby," a large and well-ventilated building formerly used as a tobacco warehouse—since it has been found politic to separate the private soldier from his commissioned superior. At the time I mention, the Northern journals were filled with accounts of barbarities practiced by the Confederates upon those whom the fate of war had placed in their hands, and I was anxious to judge for myself the correctness of these statements. Let your readers determine from my statement whether the charge of cruelty can be established: The rations which I saw distributed to the prisoners were in every respect the same as those issued to the Southern soldier; possibly the former may get more fresh meat; and that, I apprehend, is scarcely a ground for objection. They certainly do not get such luxuries as coffee or sugar, but the Confederates are no better off with respect to these condiments, which, indeed are only to be procured in the Southern States at such ruinous blockade prices as to prevent their finding their way into the commissariat of the Southern army. The doctor's report on the day I visited the island, will also serve to indicate that the treatment to which the prisoners are subjected is not such as to affect their health. I am convinced your readers will be astounded when I tell them that out of 7000 of these cruelly-*used captives, the sick-list only gave 13 in hospital. Why, I have known, in one morning's report, as many as seventy-five or a hundred to be returned as unfit for duty out of a skeleton brigade of fifteen hundred in Bragg's army. After six months' confinement of these Federal prisoners at Belle Isle, there were only seventy-five graves to indicate the number of those who had died under the privations to which they are said to have been subjected! Any*

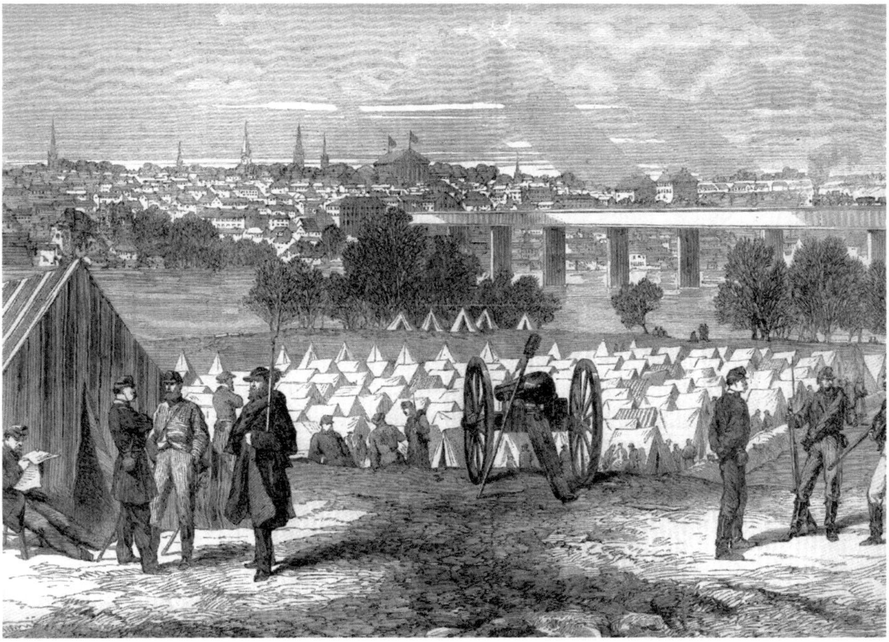

Camp of Federal prisoners on Belle Isle across the river from Richmond.

Adjutant-General of a division of 5000 men in Lee's army could show a very different bill of mortality from sickness and hardship embracing a corresponding period. I think that these statements should go a great way to disprove the charges made by the Northern press. The Northern journals have undoubtedly been misinformed on this particular, and it is only an act of justice on my part to dispel from your readers' minds any wrong impressions they may have formed as to the treatment which the Federal prisoners meet at the hands of the Confederates.

While in Richmond, Vizetelly decided to return to his native country. Pondering leaving Virginia and his Confederate friends, he wrote thoughtfully of his relationships with the generals and soldiers he had grown to respect:

Many a gallant deed and many a well-fought field that I had witnessed with my Southern friends were reviewed rapidly... There curled the blue smoke from the tent of Robert E. Lee, whose hand I had just shaken, and whose friendship I am proud to own; there were the quarters of the gallant Stuart, whose guest I had been for the past few days and whose hospitality in the field I had enjoyed for many months. Yes, every soldier of the Army of Northern Virginia was a comrade; we marched many weary miles together, and I had shared in some of their dangers. This brought me nearer to them than years of ordinary contact could have done.; and now, as I look on their camp for perhaps the last time, I realized painfully and forcibly the many friends who were lying there, some of whom would breathe their last in the first glad sunshine of coming spring. Not only did I survey the camp of the living, but around me, on every side as far as the eye could reach, lay spread the battle-fields of Virginia; and in many a distant clump of pine wood sleep those whom I had known in life. Requiescat in pace. *Far away in the background tipped with snow, towered the mountains of the Blue Ridge, every pass of which bears the imprint of the dead hero, Stonewall Jackson, and of the gallant men who fought with him in the valley of the Shenandoah that lies beyond. Through these passes were made some of those wonderful flank movements which for clerity* [sic] *and success have challenged the admiration of the world.*

There, within the eye's glance, lay a classic ground, crimsoned with deeds that will make history for the future. The camp which now looked so calm and peaceful in the winter's sunshine, with naught to disturb the quiet but the stroke of the pioneer's axe cutting fuel for the bivouac fire, would in a few short weeks be broken up.

Across the Rapidan, which flows beyond the nearer crest of hills, lay the enemy, only waiting probably the first approach of spring to renew the awful drama that has spread desolation over many a once smiling acre of Virginia soil. As I grasped the hands of my friends at their leavetaking, they know that the present lull was but a forerunner of a coming storm; every man and here, dispassionately, will I assert that, whatever be the result of the approaching campaign, I am confident that General Lee and his veterans will have done their duty. And now, while bidding farewell to an army with which I have been associated for a lengthened period, let me take an opportunity of thanking all those officers and soldiers whose guest I have been during my sojourn in the Confederacy. From the Rappahannock to the banks of the Yazoo in Mississippi, from Tennessee to the Atlantic seaboard, every detachment, every Southern command, has received me with unvarying courtesy and whole-souled hospitality; what they have had has been cheerfully shared with your correspondent. To procure me facilities great warriors and "medicine men" have not hesitated to inconvenience themselves where necessary, and if your readers have not benefited as they might have done by my experiences, it is the fault of a rigorous blockade which has intercepted much destined for your pages.

Chapter 12

Coming Home?

At the end of January 1864, Vizetelly left Richmond for Wilmington. There he booked passage on British blockade runner *Hansa* for Nassau, the mainstay of Anglo-Confederate naval operations. As was typical, the captain of the *Hansa* had to evade Northern cruisers en route. When he arrived in Nassau, Vizetelly wrote about the operations at the port:

> *The enterprise of British merchants has lined its quays with long light-coloured, rakish looking steamers, discharging their rich freights of cotton that have run the gauntlet through the Federal cruisers off Wilmington. The voyage from the Confederate States averages about fifty hours; but then these fifty hours are fraught with an excitement that a voyage of fifty days would fail in producing. From the time of leaving Cape Fear River, Wilmington, to the time of sighting Nassau and getting into the British waters, these adventurous crafts are never safe from being overhauled by a Northern man-of-war. Many a feat of heroism has been displayed by the plucky Englishmen who command them, and I have known instances of a vessel being chased and fired into for an entire day, and the only answer given in reply was to display the British ensign more proudly than ever… Nassau is the point whence most of the blockaders start with the cargoes destined for the Southern Confederacy, and it is here that cotton which they have obtained in exchange for the rifles, they return with their bales of Sea Island and Upland blankets and shoes so much needed by the Southern soldier. The climate of the Bahamas, of which New Providence is one of the group, is almost tropical; and pleasant, indeed, to your correspondent with the change from the wintry weather which he had experienced on the banks of the Rapidan. Oranges, shaddocks, bananas, coconuts, pineapples, and many other varieties of fruit abound, and lovely to the eye is the diversity*

> *of foliage in which the charming bungalow residences are embedded. The people of the place, led by their popular Governor and his lady, are the most hospitable I have ever met; and the officers of the 1st West India Regiment, stationed at Nassau, are the best of men it has been my chance to fall in with on a foreign station…*
>
> *We now engrave a vessel of this description lying at the wharf in Nassau unshipping her valuable freight. The thousand Negroes engaged in this labour make the neighborhood of the quays resound with their songs as they heave and haul at the heavy bales; and some, carried away by their excitement, leap on to the fluffy piles and relieve themselves by a "break down."*

Once Vizetelly completed his travel to England, he spent some time visiting friends and renewing acquaintances. He was "feted by his titled and wealthy acquaintances and warmly welcomed by his fellow-members of the Savage Club" and enjoyed dinners at the Cheshire Cheese House.

Coincidently, Vizetelly arrived at London at the same time that General Giuseppe Garibaldi, "the Hero of Italy," made his trip to England. Garibaldi was welcomed to England as a classical hero, comparable to Joan of Arc or

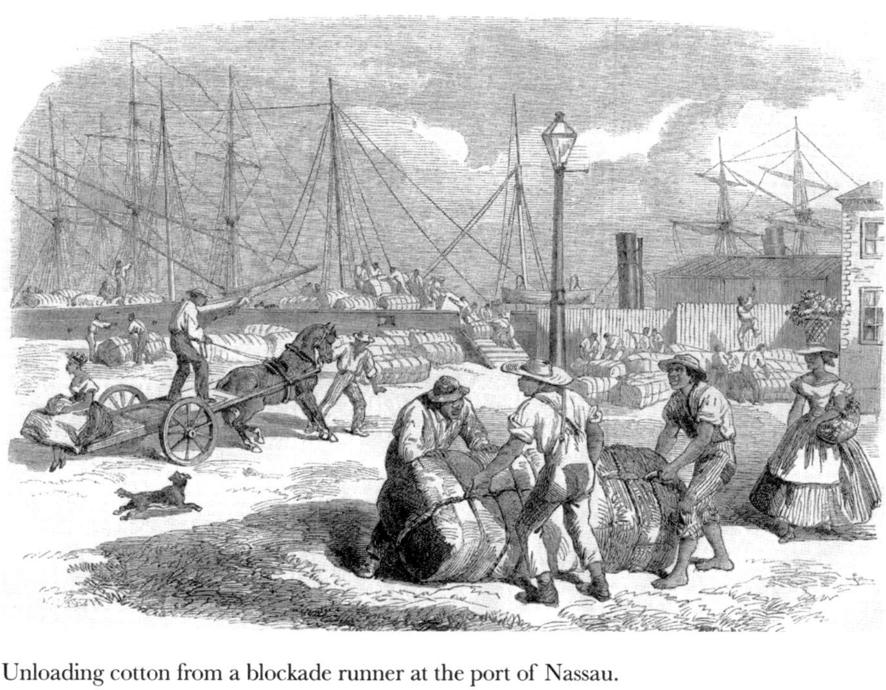

Unloading cotton from a blockade runner at the port of Nassau.

William Tell. Vizetelly enjoyed several opportunities to visit with the Italian general he covered in such detail years before.

As reassuring as it felt to be home in London, it was not long before Vizetelly begin to "pine for the exciting campaigning in the South." Joined by Francis Lawley and without even bidding goodbye to his friends or family, Vizetelly went to Southampton and sailed for Bermuda.

Reaching Bermuda, the two correspondents boarded the *Lilian*, a blockade runner captained by John Newland Maffitt and bound for Wilmington. They were accompanied on the trip by the *Florie*, another blockade runner named for Captain Maffitt's daughter. Both of the ships were new, Glasgow-built vessels of five hundred tons and perfect, low lines, and both were "painted a dull leaden gray color, to make them as invisible as possible at sea." Vizetelly sketched the ship and crew, drawing himself in the middle on deck.

Two hundred miles from Wilmington, Maffitt spotted a ship in distress, but the ship turned out to be a Federal cruiser. The captain quickly altered course and continued toward Wilmington. Nearing Wilmington, the *Lilian* was spotted by a Federal cruiser and Maffitt stoked the steam pressure "as the revolutions of the paddle mounted from twenty-six to twenty-eight to

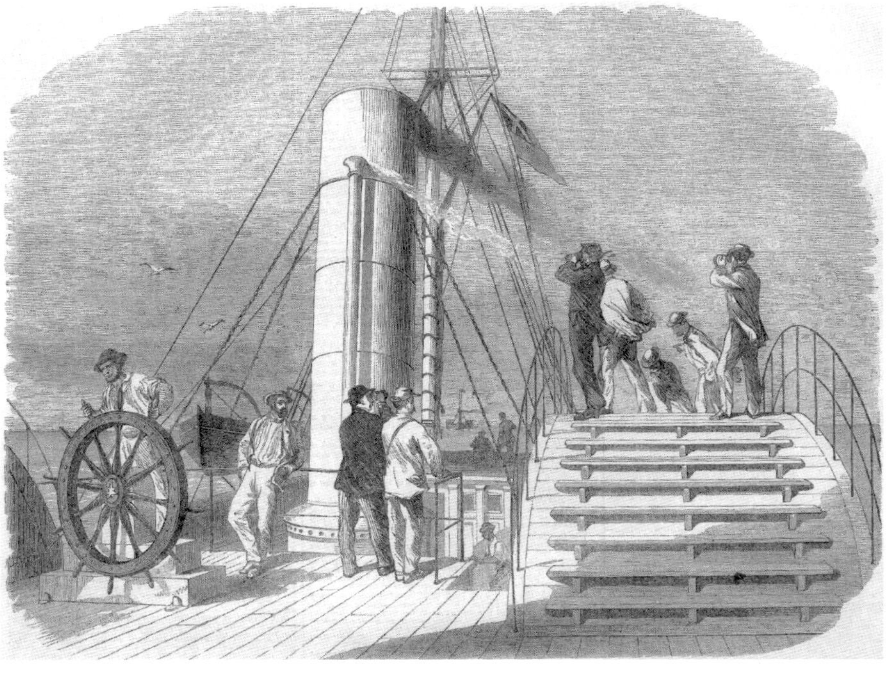

Onboard the *Lilian*, running the blockade into Wilmington Harbor.

thirty-three per minute, the *Lilian* flew out to sea swift as an arrow from a bow." They eluded the Federal ship, Vizetelly noted.

> *This also the light-heeled* Lilian *had little difficulty in accomplishing but as the sun dropped into the sea, and our pursuer, although distant, still hung upon our rear, we found that, reckoning little the speed of our advance, we had sighted the inside blockade squadron before the close of day. There was nothing for it but to persevere, and fortunately, before we approached close to land, darkness had completely set in. Silently and with bated breath we passed cruiser after cruiser, distinctly visible to every eye, and suggesting the flashing out a blue or Drummond light, and the rush of grape-shot and shrapnel through our rigging and bulwarks. But it was not destined that upon this occasion the* Lilian *should receive her baptism of fire. Just as we approach Fort Fisher a dark spot is seen on the bar. It is a Federal launch, seen by us too late for Captain Maffitt to indulge the anxious wish of his heart, and to run her down. We pass her within twenty yards, and again the expected volley of musketry is wanting. Another moment and we are under the mound upon which stands the fort, and early questioned for news… Three hours after up come the* Florie, *and is heavily fired at as she wears inwards. But the morning finds both vessels and their cargoes safe at their wharf in Wilmington, nor is it rash to predict for them the probability of many returns. At least it may safely be augured that it will take no ordinary amount of speed and courage to circumvent so fearless and experienced a sailor as Captain Maffitt, and that in his new career his skill and success will be not inferior to those which he exhibited in his old.*

It was June 4, 1864, when the *Lilian* arrived at port in Wilmington. Vizetelly and Lawley immediately left for Virginia, now his home away from home. Two weeks later, he joined Longstreet's corps at Petersburg. He witnessed the Texans from the corps retaking the outer entrenchments on the south side of the James River:

> *At first, General Anderson who, in the absence of General Longstreet from the field, commanded the corps, thought it necessary to storm the position, and gave orders to Pickett's division to go in. Immediately afterwards it was discovered that we could get a better line without sacrificing the men, and the order to assault was countermanded, but too late; for Pickett was already at it. Field's division, however, was pulled up, as it was on its way*

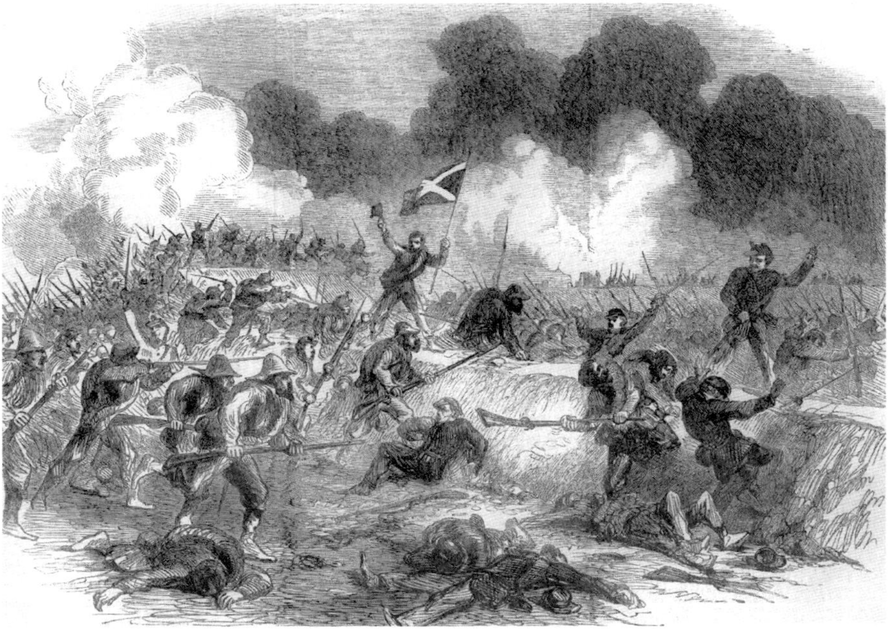

The Texans of Longstreet's corps retaking the outer lines of intrenchments on the south side of the James River.

to support the other; and aides-de-camp were sent to recall Pickett. In the meantime, Field's Texans got impatient. They straggled to the front by twos and threes, despite every effort to keep them back. At last, the whole body, officers and men, gave a yell, and with one rush they were in the works. The Yankees fled pell-mell to a line of intrenchment [sic] *beyond, leaving heaps of dead and dying.*

Several days later, Stokes's division and others were sent across the James River to meet Grant on his approach to Petersburg. Vizetelly recorded:

Its march formed the most picturesque scene I have ever witnessed. The woods had caught fire in many places from shells throw into them, and the bright flames leapt up the tall trees, casting a ruddy glare upon the faces of those careless warriors as they passed under the fire-branches, which were dropping flakes of fire. Now and then an old shell would explode in the undergrowth; but this was looked upon as an enlivening incident, with which the men were rather pleased. The woods about Bottom's Bridge are filled with dead Federals,

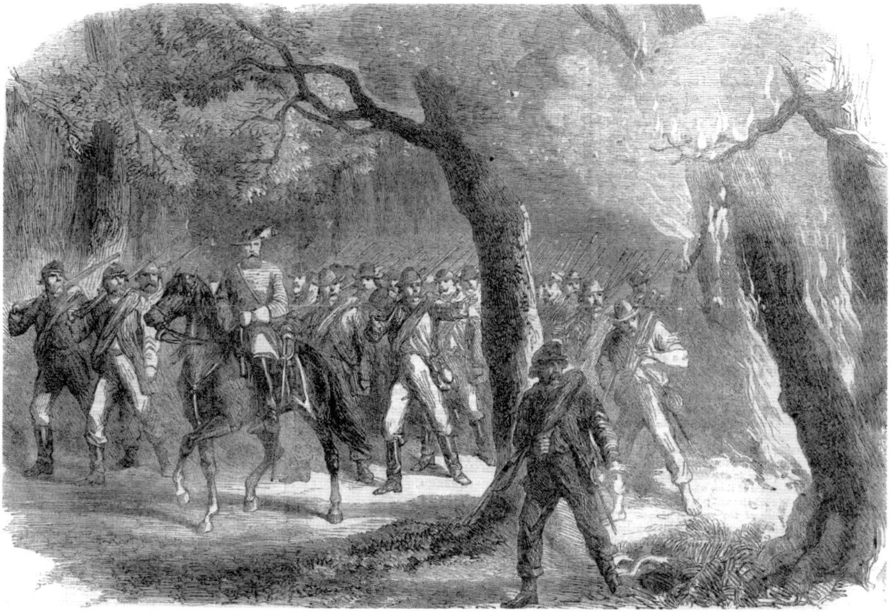

The Confederate army marching by night through the burning woods to Petersburg.

> *whom their humane commander, General Grant has left unburied. Perhaps the burning of the timber in which these corpses lie will save Richmond from a pestilence they would otherwise create. For miles outside the works of Richmond you meet with such fearful traces of the slaughter which the Federals suffered in their unsuccessful efforts to break through the Confederate lines.*

Vizetelly made several sketches of the town of Petersburg. At the beginning of the war, Petersburg had a population of twelve thousand and held several large cotton and tobacco warehouses. Interestingly, Petersburg was the hometown of Union general Winfield Scott.

Vizetelly's second sketch was drawn from General Lee's headquarters. Lee is depicted on the right side of the engraving. Vizetelly reported:

> *The shell-firing from the Federal side has been entirely bestowed upon the women and children who still remained in the town, and that it had not done the slightest injury to the Confederate troops, who were lying snug enough in their trenches beyond the belt of wood which surrounds Petersburg. The men of the advanced posts on both sides would sometimes leave off shooting at each other, come forward, and have a friendly talk.*

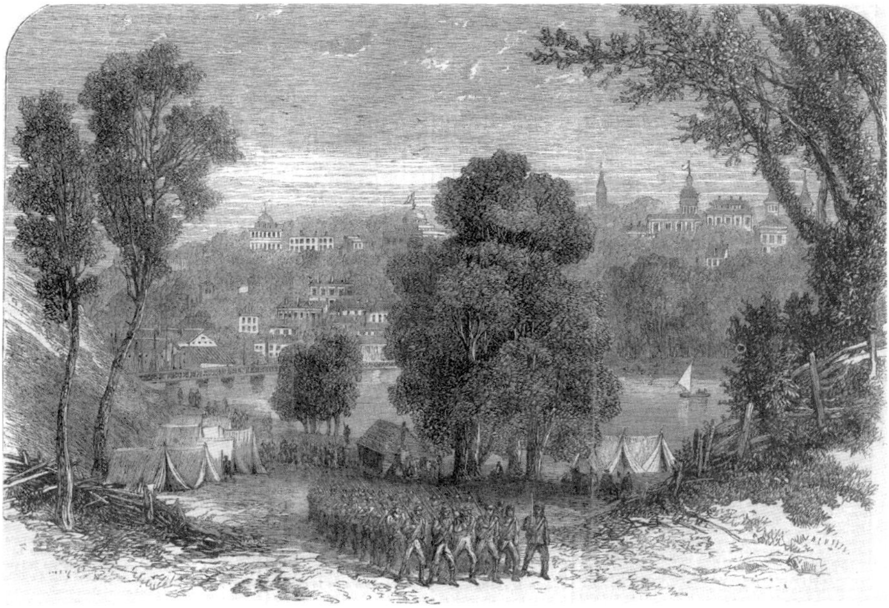

The town of Petersburg, Virginia.

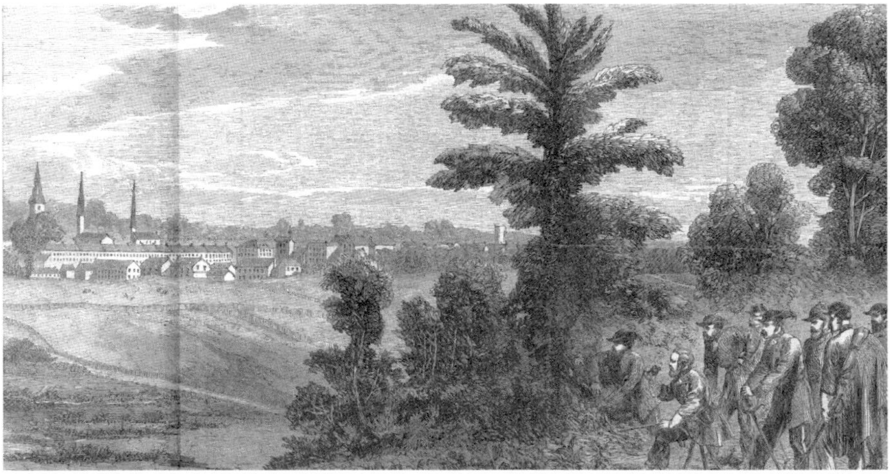

The view of Petersburg from General Lee's headquarters.

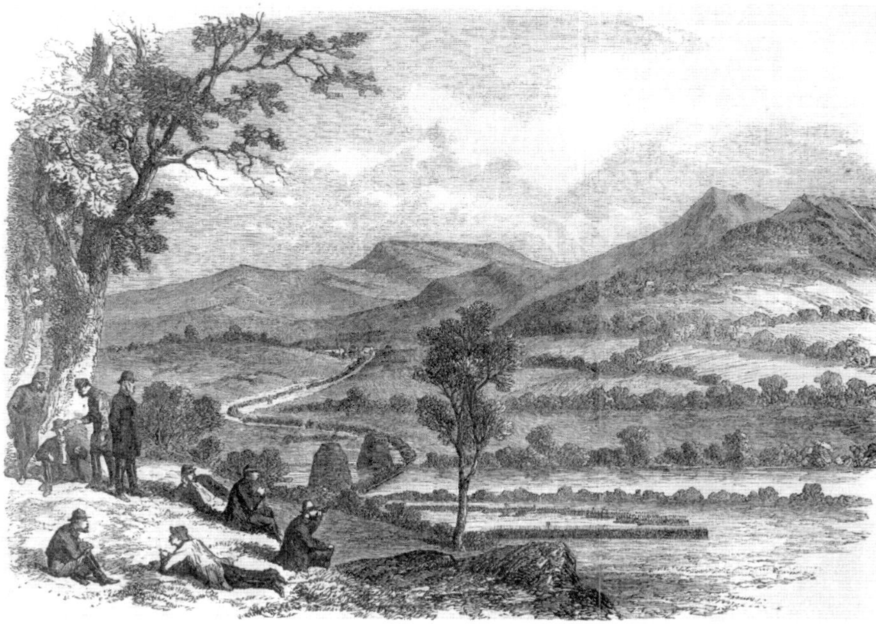

Passage up the Shenandoah River at Front Royal by Confederate divisions to reinforce General Early.

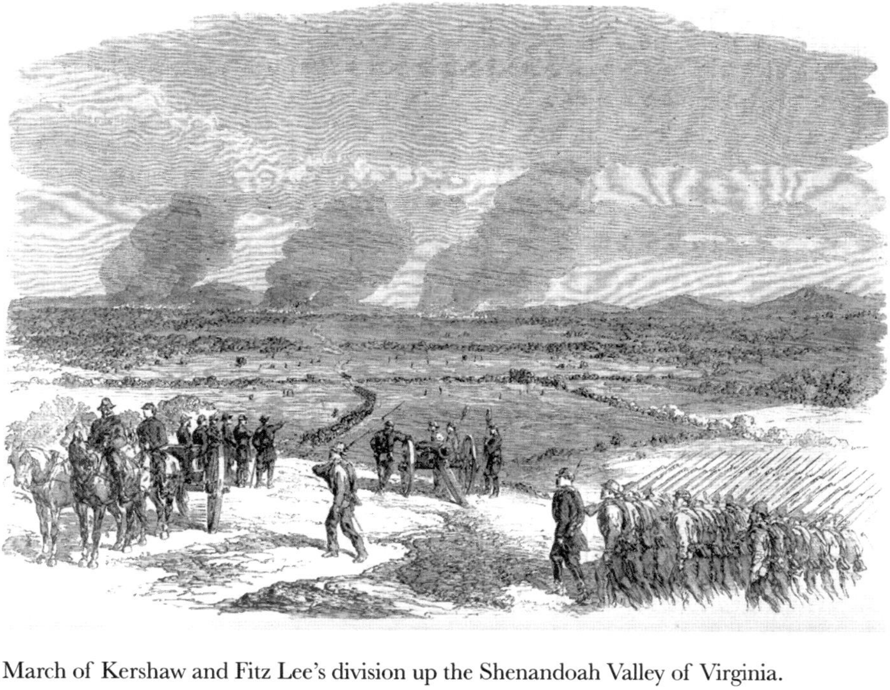

March of Kershaw and Fitz Lee's division up the Shenandoah Valley of Virginia.

After Petersburg, Vizetelly traveled to the Shenandoah Valley. Several of his sketches did make it through the blockade to England—including Confederate divisions passing the Shenandoah River to reinforce General Early, and the march of Kershaw and Fitz Lee's divisions up the valley of Virginia.

The reporter noted that "the Federals retreated, burning and laying waste every homestead in their track; thereby reducing hundreds of families to absolute poverty and possible starvation." The devastation in the Shenandoah Valley was so complete, the newspaper reported that "a crow flying across the once-fair valley would now have to carry his own rations with him."

While in the Shenandoah Valley, Vizetelly met Colonel John S. Mosby. Nicknamed the "Gray Ghost," Mosby commanded the Forty-third Battalion of the First Virginia Cavalry, a group noted for its daring raids on the Union positions and supply lines. Vizetelly sketched the famous unit at the rendezvous in the Blue Ridge Mountains:

> *To my mind, he* [Mosby] *is the most astonishing guerilla leader in the Confederacy; and the tales one hears of him sound more like the romance of*

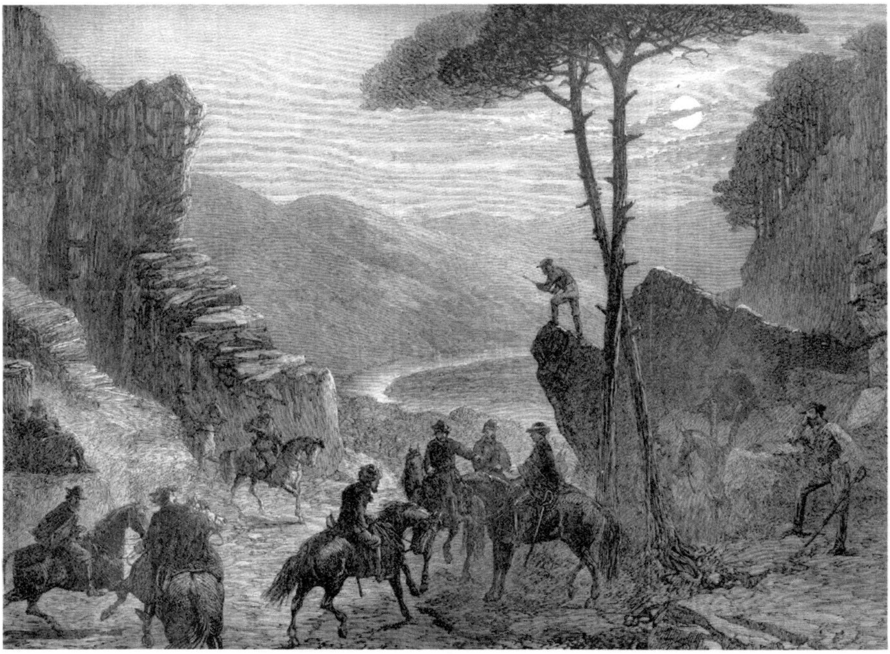

Rendezvous of Mosby's men in the pass of the Blue Ridge Mountains, Shenandoah Valley.

> *war than the reality; but when it is considered how few men he usually attacks with, his achievements are perfectly marvelous. With comparatively a handful of troops, he does not hesitate to dash on a train of two or three thousand waggons, fighting and dispersing a guard four or five times his number, and appropriating to the use of the Confederacy the supplies and transportation intended for Sheridan's army. At other times he will fly at much higher game, piercing the centre of a large column on the march, and before either the van or rear are aware of the cause of the momentary tumult, he will be flying to the mountains with a goodly number of prisoners. It is impossible to describe the terror that he excites amongst the Federals; and whenever a party of them are moving through the valley they are most eager in the inquiries as to whether Mosby is anywhere in the neighborhood. Of course they get little information from the inhabitants, whose idol he is. Originally, Mosby's band consisted of but one company but it has lately been raised to a thousand, and he himself made a colonel in the Confederate army, though none of his soldiers are regularly enlisted soldiers. They are mostly sons of farmers and gentlemen, who prefer the ubiquitous life and its stirring adventures offered by their chieftain to the comparative monotony of the ranks in a Virginia regiment. They receive no pay from the War Office, but, instead of it, they are allowed to dispose of their captures for their own benefit, the Government being the purchaser. As soon as an expedition has been resolved upon, Mosby sends a summons to his men, who are dispersed in every direction, to meet him at some gap in the mountains, generally at night, and few fail to answer the call. If they should do so three times consecutively they are immediately handed over to the authorities and conscribed into the regular army.*

Just before Christmas 1864, Vizetelly once again bid Virginia farewell and left to cover the Union attempts to capture Fort Fisher near Wilmington. The fort, nicknamed the "Gibraltar of the Confederacy," was protected by a ten-foot parapet. It contained fifty heavy cannons. The Confederate garrison there consisted of 1,400 troops commanded by Colonel William Lamb. With Charleston bottled up with the Federal blockade, Wilmington was the last seaport open to blockade runners and the last means of supply for the Army of Northern Virginia.

On Christmas morning, thousands of Union soldiers landed on the sandy approach to Fort Fisher but were driven back. The Union forces regrouped, and on January 13, a joint naval and land assault of Fort Fisher commenced. The fleet included fifty-two ships and carried ten thousand troops.

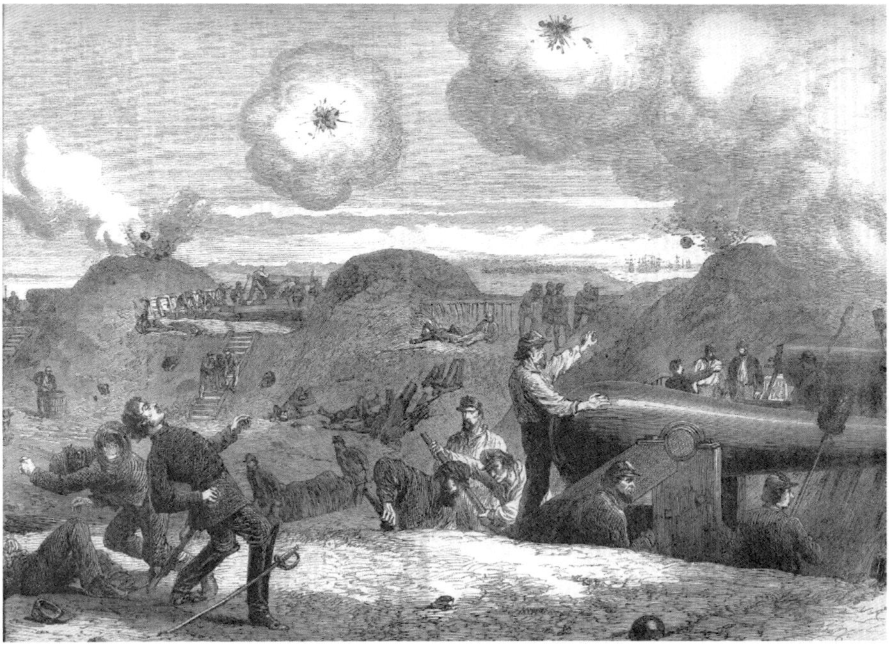

Interior of Fort Fisher near Wilmington during the bombardment.

The Union troops, under Major General Alfred Terry, landed between Hoke and Fort Fisher on the thirteenth and spent the next day moving south toward Fort Fisher. On the fifteenth, the Union gunboats opened fire. Vizetelly sketched the fight from the vantage point of Fort Fisher:

> *A part of the Federal fleet is seen lying at anchor towards the right-hand side of this view; while the storming party, which numbered 2500 men, is landing in the distance and preparing to extend itself across the neck of land between the sea and Cape Fear River. The guns in the battery, shown in the right-hand corner of the foreground, are still being worked against that part of the Federal fleet which lies father to the right, and which cannot, therefore, be included in this view. Most of the others, guns in the fort have been disabled by the heavy shot of the enemy; and the exposed position of the men, with shells of the largest size falling and exploding in the midst of them, is terribly apparent in our illustration.*

With the defeat of Fort Fisher, Vizetelly returned to Richmond. With no seaport still open for the Confederacy, he had no means to send this sketches and reports out to London. He remained in Virginia until April 2 and then slipped away to join General Joe Johnston and his army in North Carolina. He was with Johnston at the Battle of Bentonville, at which he stated he "saw the last shot of the war fired." After Johnston's surrender, there was no standing Confederate army left east of the Mississippi.

Chapter 13

Government in Exile

Vizetelly boarded a train at Durham's Station and traveled to Greensboro hoping to intercept President Davis fleeing south after the fall of Richmond.

Without Vizetelly's illustrations for print, the *Illustrated London News* relied on engravings of Lincoln's second inauguration and stories of the assassination and funeral. The newspaper also ran stories of Jefferson Davis's flight south, but no one had any images to print. There were many rumors that made the paper, including stories that Davis had reached Texas en route to Mexico.

Vizetelly's instincts were correct—Davis was heading south to avoid capture. On Sunday, April 2, Davis and all but one of his cabinet members gathered at the Richmond-Danville Railroad Depot. At approximately 11:00 p.m., the train departed. In the president's car was Secretary of State Judah P. Benjamin, Secretary of the Navy Stephen R. Mallory, Secretary of the Treasury George A. Trenholm and his wife, Attorney General George Davis and Postmaster General John H. Reagan. Secretary of War General John Breckinridge stayed behind to supervise the evacuation of Richmond.

Also on the train was a group of sixty handpicked midshipmen from the Confederate Naval Academy led by Captain William H. Parker. Parker and his sailors were escorting $500,000 in gold nuggets, coins and silver bars, the last of the Confederate treasury.

The next day, the train arrived at Danville, Virginia, taking eighteen hours to make the 140-mile trip. With Union general Stoneman driving toward Danville, Grant pursuing Lee in Virginia and Sherman facing Johnston in North Carolina, the noose was tightening around the Confederacy.

On April 10, Davis's train pulled out of Virginia and headed to Greensboro, fifty miles away. Reaching Greensboro, Trenholm, who was ill, left the train. While it was paused at Greensboro, Breckinridge caught up with the group.

In a cabinet meeting on April 12, Davis made it clear that his intention was to fight on. He informed the group that he hoped to travel to the Southwest to meet General Edmund Kirby-Smith, who was still commanding an army in the West.

Unknown to his editors, Vizetelly did find Davis and his entourage in North Carolina as his train pulled into Greensboro on April 15. Davis was informed that Stoneman had destroyed the railroad line south of Greensboro, leaving the group no choice but to proceed on horseback.

An escort of Tennessee and Kentucky cavalry, under the command of Brigadier General George D. Dibrell, arrived to serve as Davis's escort. A group of horses and carriages was assembled for the Confederate officials. With the necessary transportation assembled, the group pulled out of Greensboro in a long line of horsemen, cavalry, infantry, ambulances and wagons, with Davis at the lead. Vizetelly was the only correspondent to accompany the group.

While in Lexington, North Carolina, Davis wrote his wife that "if only a devoted band of cavalry will cling to me…I can force my way across the Mississippi and go to Mexico and have the world from whence to choose a location."

Near Salisbury, North Carolina, Davis's party faced a major challenge for a large group with so many horses and vehicles—the crossing of the Pee Dee River. Vizetelly sketched the tedious operation getting a large group to cross a swift river. Each wagon had to be ferried across separately. The horses had to be stripped of their saddles and swim across as they were coaxed by their riders. Vizetelly did note that he was dunked in the river several times in the crossing.

By May 1, the presidential party had made its way across South Carolina. Ready to cross into Georgia, Vizetelly sketched one of the many times that the group was alarmed by the potential of a Union regiment locating them:

> *Our readers must bear in mind that at any moment the alarm might be given of the enemy's advance, and, to say the least, such a condition of matters was scarcely calculated to give calmness to the deliberations of the fugitive Government.*
>
> *The subject of another illustration is the scene presented by a sudden alarm, or stampede, which was a very frequent occurrence, owing to the proximity of the Federal cavalry, who were frequently within three miles of the camp of the flying President. A scout only had to dash in and give*

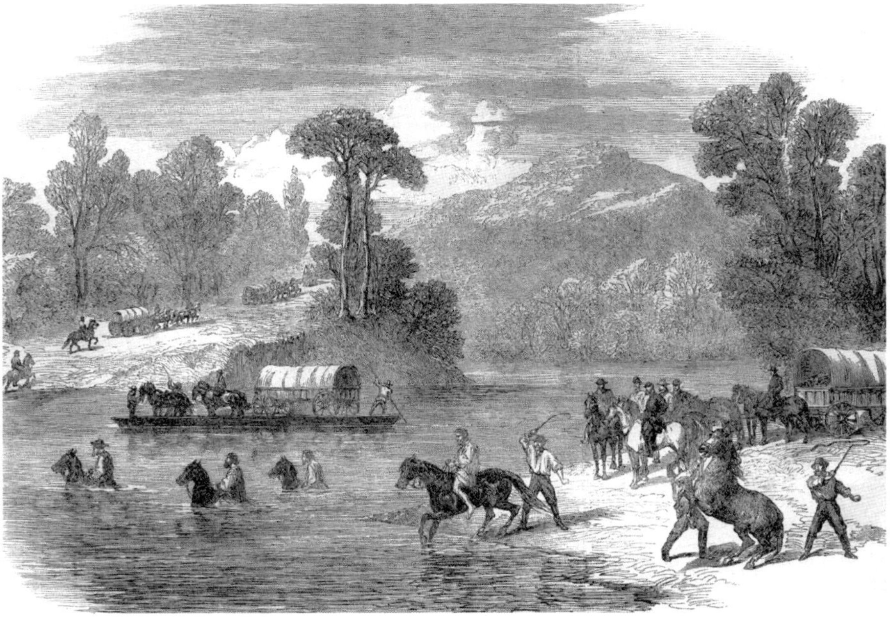

President Davis's train crossing the Pee Dee River in North Carolina.

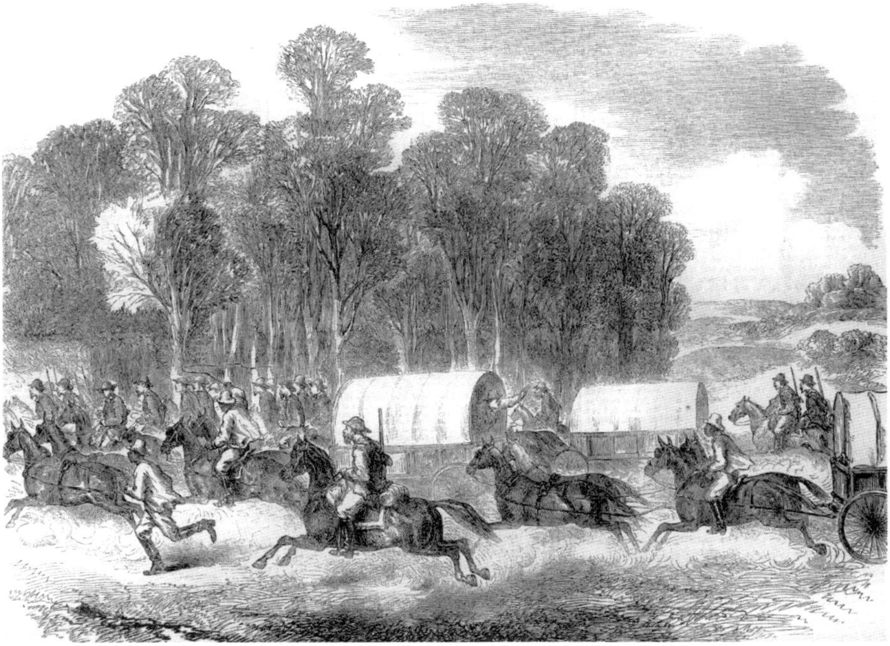

A sudden alarm as the Federal cavalry neared Davis's group.

> *the alarm when everything went helter-skelter along the road—President, Ministers, cavalrymen, four-muled waggons, and terrified Negro servants, all jumbled up together.*

In another illustration, Vizetelly sketched Davis executing his signature on several documents presented to him by Secretary of State Benjamin. He observed:

> *This was probably the last official business transacted by the Confederate Cabinet and may well be termed "Government by the roadside." Our readers must bear in mind that at any moment the alarm might be given of the enemy's advance, and, to say the least, such a condition of matters was scarcely calculated to give calmness to the deliberations of the fugitive Government.*

On May 2, the presidential party crossed into Georgia, and without accommodations, Davis and his cabinet slept under the Georgia pines. Vizetelly sketched his next illustration as the group crossed the Georgia Ridge—"a range of wooded hills forming the boundary line of the State

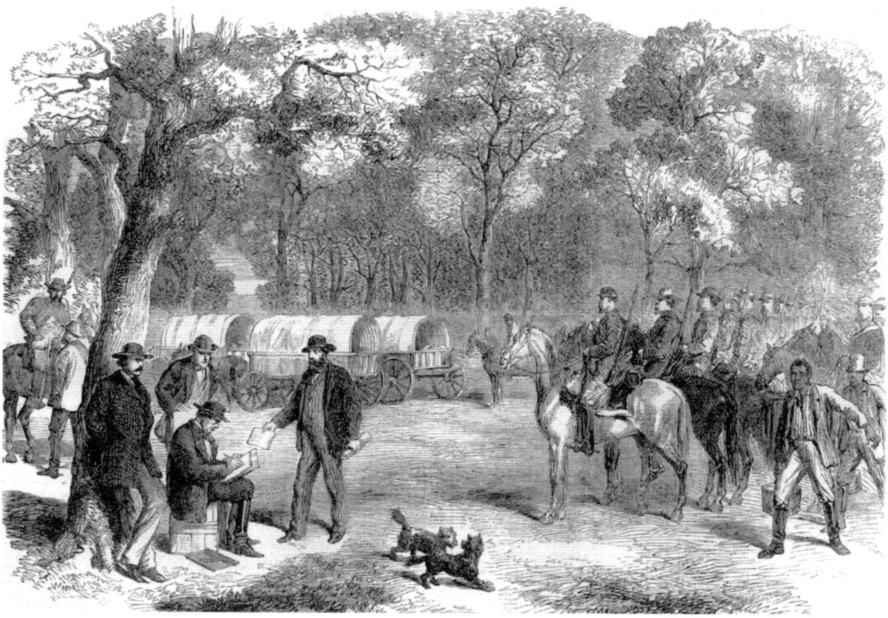

President Davis signing acts of government by the roadside.

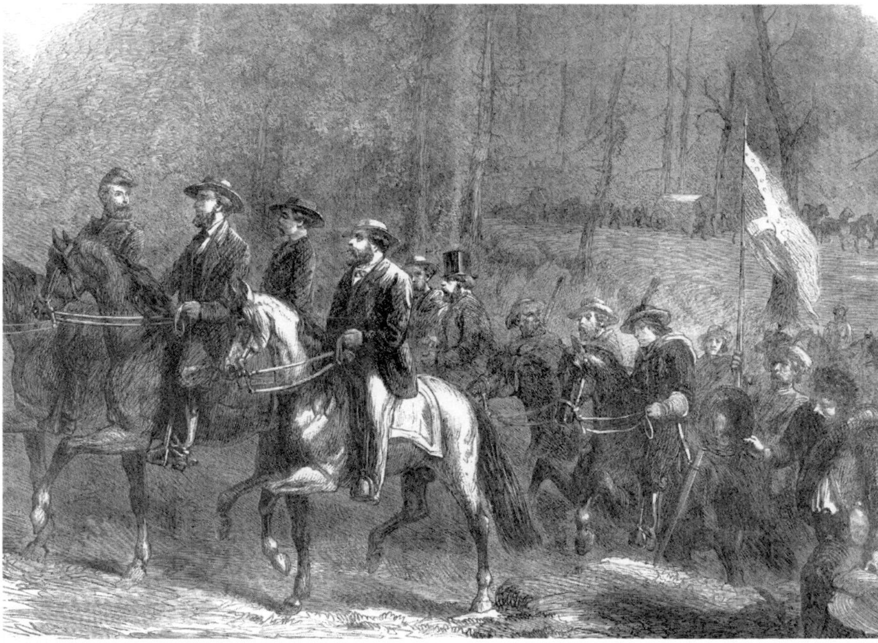

Flight of Confederate president Davis and his cabinet in Macon, Georgia.

of South Carolina." The *Illustrated London News* identified the men in the engraving as noted by their reporter: "Mr. Davis is the central figure of the three horsemen riding in front; General Bragg is on his right hand, and Mr. Benjamin, his Secretary of State, on the left; behind Mr. Davis, and on his right hand, is General Breckenridge; next to whom is Mr. Reagan, the Postmaster-General; the rest of the party are the staff of Mr. Davis and the Kentucky soldiers of his escort."

With Federal cavalry scouts pressing the entourage from all points, it was clear that the large group could no longer travel without being discovered. At Washington, Georgia, on May 4, with tears in his eyes, Davis bade farewell to all of his men, save a few companions.

He shook hands with his cabinet members and cavalry officers one by one. He then disbanded the official guard and reduced the large travel party down to one wagon and two ambulances. Vizetelly wrote of the dramatic moment:

> *It was here that* [Davis] *determined to continue his flight almost alone; and, assembling those around him who sacrificed everything to the*

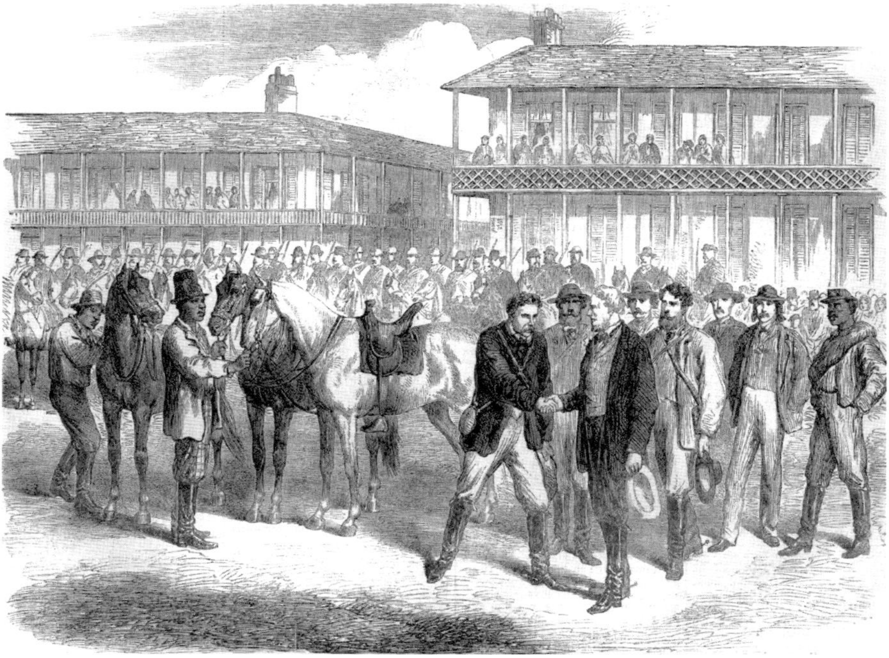

President Davis bidding farewell to his group at Washington, Georgia.

> *defeated cause, he with tears in his eyes, begged them to seek their own safety and leave him to meet his fate. Undoubtedly, it was an ill-advised arrangement which brought an escort of 1500 men in the train of a man fleeing for his life; and, when too late, Mr. Davis saw the error of this attracting the attention of the entire country through which he passed, and disbanded them.*

Davis set out with the much-reduced company, Vizetelly included, in the direction of the Florida border. The English reporter continued with Davis until Mrs. Davis joined the group near Gordon on May 9. Vizetelly donated fifty pounds to a fund to aid Davis and departed the group. He had "attended the journey of the fallen President…a distance of 700 miles… until it was disbanded, by Mr. Davis' request, before his capture."

Forty-eight hours after Vizetelly departed, Davis was captured at Irwinville, Georgia.

Epilogue

Vizetelly learned of Jefferson Davis's capture in the daily newspapers as he made his way to the coast to book passage to England. With the last chapter of the War Between the States closed, there was no reason for him to stay. While the Union still faced the long struggle to bring the nation together, as far as Vizetelly was concerned, the drama was over.

He carried his sketches and reports of Davis's flight with him to personally deliver them to the newspaper. The tired reporter, the quintessential war correspondent, the consummate journeyman—arrived in England in June. In the July 1 issue, the editor of the *Illustrated London News* announced that the Vizetelly series "The Last Days of the Confederacy" would be published in the upcoming issues, asserting that the engraving "cannot fail to prove of much interest to our readers."

During the course of the war, the *Illustrated London News* published 133 engravings attributed to Frank Vizetelly. *Harper's Weekly* frequently published Vizetelly's work as well—some that were simply copied by artists from the pages of the London newspaper, others that were captured and sold to the New York newspaper of Union soldiers and sailors. Many illustrations and reports never made it to either newspaper, perhaps discarded as worthless by the men aboard a Federal cruiser focusing on the more valuable booty seized on a blockade runner. Others likely rest at the bottom of the sea, trapped in a ship that refused to yield to the blockade.

The mark of any great reporter or war correspondent, Vizetelly always had a great instinct—a nose for news. However, in a war fought on so many fronts, in which wartime transportation was neither quick nor reliable, he made choices about where to locate. He was outside of Vicksburg with Joe Johnston's army when Lee was defeated at Gettysburg. Vizetelly was in Charleston when Lee and Jackson pulled off perhaps a flawless battle, defeating an army twice their size. Of course, missing Chancellorsville meant also missing the death of Stonewall Jackson, perhaps, other than Lee, the most iconic and revered officer of the Confederacy.

Perhaps the missed moment that Vizetelly deeply regretted was the death of General J.E.B. Stuart. Vizetelly and Stuart developed a deep affection for each other. Both were in constant search for all the adventure that life could offer. Both were gregarious, affable men who enjoyed the camaraderie offered by camp life. Most of all they enjoyed each other's company.

When Vizetelly left Virginia for England in January 1864, he said his last goodbye to his friend Stuart. When he decided to return that same spring, he most certainly looked forward to once again sharing stories and songs with the young cavalier around a campfire in Virginia. While Vizetelly was traveling across the Atlantic, returning to the Confederate States, Stuart was mortally wounded at the Battle of Yellow Tavern on May 11. He died the next day at the young age of thirty-one.

After publishing his last engravings of the war, Vizetelly took a month for a well-deserved rest and re-immersed himself in the social life of London. By August 1865, he traveled to the Isle of Valencia off the southwest coast of Ireland to cover the laying of the Atlantic telegraph cables to connect Europe and North America. Later, he covered the short-lived war between Prussia and Austria in 1866.

In the Austro-Prussian War, Vizetelly reestablished a relationship with Major Heros von Borcke of the Prussian army who rode with J.E.B. Stuart. In the war, von Borcke distinguished himself in the service to his native Prussia and received the Order of the Red Eagle for gallantry. Vizetelly agreed to illustrate a book written by von Borcke entitled *Memoirs of the Confederate War for Independence.*

With his older brother James, Vizetelly began publication of a weekly paper named *Echoes from the Clubs: A Record of Political Topics and Social Amenities.* Vizetelly produced the satirical cartoons for the paper. The venture only lasted twenty months, being crushed by the many lawsuits brought by Londoners unhappy with the coverage received.

After covering the Carlist insurrection in Spain in 1867, Vizetelly "retired," settling for several years at Hendaye, a French beach resort on the Bidassoa River. He left Hendaye, moving to Gironde on the Atlantic coast, where he sketched the many famous chateaux and vineyards in the Medac.

Though living his life in a luxurious setting, Vizetelly could never ignore the call of the adventure of war and the camaraderie of men in the field.

He was drawn to the Mahdist's insurrection against Egyptian rule in Sudan, covering the war for the London *Graphic*.

By 1883, the London newspaper was no longer receiving reports from Vizetelly. It was believed that he was killed at the massacre of British soldiers at the Battle of Kashgil in November 1883. Like his good friend J.E.B. Stuart, Vizetelly finally fell victim to his own search for adventure.

Bibliography

Blackford, W.W. *War Years with Jeb Stuart.* New York: Scribner & Sons, 1945.

Brown, Josua. *Beyond the Lines: Pictorial Reporting, Everyday Life, and the Crisis of Gilded Age America.* Berkeley: University of California Press, 2002.

Cochran, Robert T. "Witness to a War: British Correspondent Frank Vizetelly." *National Geographic* (April 1961).

Confederate Veteran 32, no. 285. "An Englishman with the Confederate Army." (July 1924).

Government Printing Office. *War of the Rebellion: A Compilation of the Official Records of the Union and Confederate Armies.* Washington, D.C.: Government Printing Office, 1880–1901.

Holsinger, M. Paul, ed. *War and American Popular Culture.* Westport, CT: Greenwood Press, 1999.

Hoole, William Stanley. *Vizetelly Covers the Confederacy.* Tuscaloosa: University of Alabama Press, 1957.

Illustrated London News, 1861–65.

Neely, Mark E., Jr., Harold Holzer and Gabor S. Boritt. *The Confederate Image: Prints of the Last Cause.* Chapel Hill: University of North Carolina Press, 2000.

Ross, Fitzgerald. *A Visit to the Cities and Camps of the Confederate States.* London: W. Blackwood and Sons, 1865.

Thompson, W. Fletcher. *The Image of War: The Pictorial Reporting of the American Civil War.* New York: Thomas Yoseloff, 1959.

Vizetelly, Frank. "Charleston Under Fire." *Cornhill Magazine* 10 (July 1864): 99–110.

Von Borcke, Heros. *Memoirs of the Confederate War for Independence.* London: Peter Smith, 1866.

Zeller, Bob. *The Blue & Gray in Black & White: A History of Civil War Photography.* Westport, CT: Praeger Publishers, 2005.

Visit us at
www.historypress.net